Northwest
WALKS

Northwest
Walks

Gary Ferguson

Illustrations and maps by Kent Humphreys
Research coordinated by Jane Ferguson

Fulcrum Publishing
Golden, Colorado

Library of Congress Cataloging-in-Publication Data

Ferguson, Gary, 1956–
    Northwest walks / by Gary Ferguson
        p.   cm.
    Includes bibliographical references and index.
    ISBN 1-55591-191-9
    1. Hiking—Northwestern States—Guidebooks.   2. Northwestern States—Description and travel.   I. Title.
GV199.42.N695F47   1995
796.5'1'0979—dc20   94-38964
                                                                        CIP

Printed in the United States of America
0   9   8   7   6   5   4   3   2

Fulcrum Publishing
350 Indiana Street, Suite 350
Golden, Colorado 80401-5093

To Ken, Bernie, Janice, Steve, John,
Cheryl, Joan, Chuck, and Brady.

And to Stanley, Idaho—the best town
this kid ever had.

· Contents ·

Contents

· Introduction ·

If I were allowed just one last, grand dance across the great natural areas of the world, certainly some of my first steps would be through the 250,000 square miles of mountains, forests, coasts, and deserts of the American Northwest. Within this vast landscape is a staggering range of ecosystems, broad and deep enough to please the most discriminating nature lover. In western Washington you'll find the largest mountain glacier system in the continental United States; a day's drive to the southeast is the deepest major river gorge on the North American continent, patiently slicing its way through the dry, tawny hills of Idaho. Here it's possible to watch the sun rise across one of the largest volcanic plateaus in the world, and by that afternoon be wrapped in a cool fern garden at the feet of a thousand-year-old forest of western redcedar and Douglas fir. In May you can walk across snow 20 feet deep in the Cascades, and then head east a short distance into a braid of parched desert canyons, hot winds hissing past their smooth, varnished walls. And there is still more: rain forests, sand dunes, estuaries, and alpine meadows; coastal blowholes and volcanic blowdowns; waterfalls, marshes, and deep glacial lakes.

Political and economic motives aside, there has always been a sense of grand possibility about the Northwest—of wild secrets waiting to be uncovered. When Captain James Cook arrived off the coast of Vancouver Island in the spring of 1778, he came as an explorer, geographer, and scientist, ultimately bent on unravelling one of the most exciting puzzles in the civilized world—that of locating the fabled Northwest Passage. Just 27 years later, when Lewis and Clark set out on their great overland journey to the Pacific, it was another trek of grand discoveries—one that would again catch the spirit of a nation.

From the adventures of early explorers, it wasn't long before people started making the decision to see the lands of the Northwest for themselves. By the time John Fremont began his trailblazing expeditions in the 1840s, interest in the region was already swelling. Some were weary from sour economic conditions, as well as a series of flood-related disasters in the Midwest. Others, though, just plain fell in love with the idea of heading west. Wealthy entrepreneur Nathaniel Wyeth, who helped popularize the route that would later become the Oregon Trail, gave a good summation of the feelings of thousands of Americans with itchy feet. "I cannot divest myself of the opinion," he wrote, "that I shall compete better with my fellow men in new and untried paths than in those which require only patience and attention."

Nor, of course, was the Northwest ever lacking in publicity. In 1839, Horace Greeley ("Go west young man!") hired writer Thomas Farnham to make a trip to the Willamette Valley and share his experiences with readers who might be interested in making a similar journey. "To conclude," Farnham says in the last paragraph of his *Wagon Train Journal*, "few portions of the globe ... are to be found so rich in soil, so diversified in surface, or so capable of being rendered the happy abode of an industrious and civilized community. ... No portion of the world beyond the tropics can be found that will yield so readily with moderate labor, to the wants of man."

Say no more. Between 1840 and 1860, more than 50,000 people made their way along that long, dusty trail from the Missouri River into Oregon Territory.

Sadly, the fevered pace at which the Northwest was settled, going in 80 years from an uncharted wilderness to a rather vigorous economic center, has not been without cost to the spirit of the land. Until very recently, conservation has not been a legacy of the Northwest. Minerals were pulled from the mines of Idaho with utter abandon, the air and water badly poisoned by smelting operations and tailings piles—many of which remain serious problems to the health of residents to this day. And while logging may well be the economic lifeblood of western Oregon and Washington, the push to cut under shorter and shorter rotation periods has turned millions of acres of rich forest into little more than tree farms. (During certain periods over the past 40 years, some tree species, such as Sitka spruce, have been harvested at more than 10 times their annual growth rate.)

Fortunately, all is not lost. The sheer vastness of this region, combined with a slowly changing philosophy of resource management, has left literally thousands of square miles of rich, unfettered landscapes open to anyone who would merely set his or her feet to walking. This book is meant to be a celebration of those places— a guide to reconnecting with the calm and the beauty, the rhythm and the rhyme that come from this good land.

To that end you'll find the walks that follow are not so much concerned with destinations as they are with journeys; indeed, the turnaround points for many are rather arbitrary. These small slices of trail were chosen not so much because they led to the biggest, tallest, or best of any one thing, but because they served as quiet, engaging introductions to the secrets that still shimmer beneath these coasts, mountains, deserts, and forests. Do note that all of the distances listed for the walks are round-trip mileages; the vast majority can be easily lengthened.

Thomas Huxley once said that to a person unfamiliar with natural history, "his country or seaside stroll is a walk through a gallery filled with wonderful works of art, nine-tenths of which have their faces to the wall." And yet real familiarity with the natural world—the kind that not only feeds the head but also the heart—is to a great extent based simply on your own personal relationship with nature, on what Thoreau once described as being "conscious of a friendliness." This book is meant to take you to places where such friendships come easy—where the land is alive, and the ground rolls easily underfoot.

The Coast

I always leave this primitive beach reluctantly. The music of the ocean front seems to establish a rhythm in man. For hours and even days afterward I can almost hear the booming of the tides on the headlands and the sound of the wind in the giant spruce. ...
—*William O. Douglas*,
at Olympic National Park

It seems that there is almost no ill feeling, no worry or wave of hopelessness that the coast of Oregon and Washington cannot ease. Here are long curls of sand to walk down on bright blue days, and furious, wind-driven waves that rip to shreds the dullness we've accumulated in the trenches of the city. Here are shimmering tide pools with all the strangeness of Alice's looking glass, and estuaries that each autumn shudder with the rise and fall of beating wings. Strangely, it seems that the coast is the one ecosystem that no matter how long we spend in it we can never fully know—that place where the minds of men and women loose their moorings, drift out, and are lost to the visions of the earth.

Perhaps what is most surprising about coastal environments is how many different habitats are squeezed into a relatively small space. There are foredunes, capped with soft lines of sea rocket and silky beach pea. Along the leading edges of sand spits are the playgrounds of whales and harbor seals, while the trailing edges mark safe winter harbor for black brants, arctic loons, bufflehead, goldeneyes, scaups, teals, pintails, and Canada geese.

In the tidal pools the habitats are compressed even further. Suddenly life is balanced along the narrowest of bands: for many kinds of creatures, to move even a few yards closer to or farther from the sea would mean certain disaster. (Because of this precarious existence, it's extremely important that you put any tide pool rocks you may have moved back exactly the way you found them. What's more, never disturb eggs of any kind.)

Whether you dive into these mysteries with books and binoculars blazing, or come for nothing but an ocean sunset; whether you spend weeks prowling this maze of hidden coves and pocket beaches, or just stand beside Highway 101 for five minutes letting the rhythms of the waves roll across your shoulders, the Northwest coast will leave your world a little broader, a little brighter than it was before.

The Desert

A thousand fantasies
Begin to throng into my memory,
Of calling shapes, and beck'ning shadows dire,
And airy tongues that syllable men's names
On sands and shores and desert wildernesses.

—*John Milton*

America has been slow to warm to its fabulous array of deserts. For years we dropped bombs on such places and used them to test our atomic weapons; overgrazed their native grasses and buried our nuclear waste in their folds, sure that no one would ever care. The deserts have long been, and to some people remain even now, unfortunate landscapes—places made ugly simply through their lack of human amenities. And of all the American deserts, perhaps the Great Basin, whose fringes extend into southeastern Oregon and southern Idaho, has been appreciated least of all.

Of course, if you've spent much time here, if your senses have been honed to pick the precious from among the overwhelming, you know that these arid lands are rather amazing places. Here are the rugged, cobbled canyons where young golden eagles take their first daring leaps into the sky. Out this way are the thin canvases of earth that in spring explode with the reds of skyrockets and paintbrush; the lemons of primrose, balsamroot, and sunray; the ivories of sego lily, fleabane, and pincushion. And cradling all of it is silence and space almost beyond imagining.

Though engaging in their own right, perhaps what adds so much delight to the deserts of southeastern Oregon and southern Idaho is the fact that they're framed by such contrasting landscapes. The shimmering black basalt desert of Craters of the Moon seems more profound when backed to the north by a line of snowcapped peaks—the distant mountains approaching, as William Merwin once described it, like sails from a wingless kingdom. From the hot sands of Oregon's Alvord Desert rises the mammoth 9,733-foot Steens Mountain, while a short distance to the northwest is a braid of marsh, lake, and rimrock comprising one of the richest bird sanctuaries in America.

As you walk through the high deserts of the Northwest, look for some of the themes that serve as clues to what desert life is really about. Notice the small leaves, as well as how many of them are covered with fine hairs—both of which help conserve water. See how a landscape that may seem almost devoid of animals during the day becomes filled with activity under the cool blanket of darkness. Notice the number of burrows you see in the ground—homes that prove cool in summer and warm in winter.

Many ecologists claim that most of the country of southeastern Oregon and southern Idaho is not really a desert at all, but rather a steppe climate. The moisture in this region, they point out, is generally sufficient to support a greater volume (though not necessarily variety) of shrubs, forbes, and grasses than is typically found in the drier reaches of land that lie to the south. Certainly this is true. Indeed, were it not for the fact that most of the moisture in this region falls here in the winter, when plants are dormant and can't take full advantage of it, much of this landscape would not resemble a desert at all, but rather a lush prairie, rippling with grass.

Many of the walks that follow do indeed stretch the formal definition of desert. But what I hope will surface when you visit these places is a sense of the fabulous economy that occurs in arid lands in general. Most of us would probably agree with the old notion that nature doesn't do anything without purpose. But nowhere does that purposefulness seem more evident than when you plant yourself in a dry, thirsty landscape, where the margins of life and death have been shaved to such clean, fine lines.

The Forest

To a great many lovers of the out-of-doors, the term "Northwest" is another word for trees—trails through vast sweeps of western hemlock and Douglas fir, gentle flows of red alder running like dappled gray rivers down the lowland valleys to the sea, hushed groves of western redcedar spiked by the soft flutter of maple leaves. Filling in as background for these daydreams are lush cloaks of shrubs and flowers: huckleberry, ocean spray, rhododendron, currant, and blackberry; trillium, violets, buttercups, pipsissewa, and false lily-of-the-valley. For the most part, our fantasies of the Northwest are rich and fertile ones, reflections of the fact that in certain portions of this region can be found what are arguably the most beautiful, most diverse coniferous forests in the world.

Besides the obvious beauty of such places, perhaps there's reassurance to be found in a land that can sprout trees like winter wheat, a land that provides its wild inhabitants with such feasts of berries and insects and seeds. Much of this great gush of life is, as you might have guessed, thanks to the influence of the sea. The Pacific Ocean moderates temperatures, as well as delivers oodles of moisture in the form of rain, snow, and fog. It's these conditions that allow life in the great forests to run with such apparant abandon, to achieve the ultimate expression of the forest primeval.

Six of the dozen most common conifers in a Northwest coastal forest live for 500 years—a rate of longevity almost unheard of anywhere else. Even the shortest-lived species—the grand fir—can hang on for an impressive 300 years.

Once you move away from the coast, past the rugged wall of Cascade Mountains that grab so much moisture from the skies—once you lose the temperature-moderating effects of the ocean—the complexion of the Northwest forests changes dramatically. We find instead the stately ponderosa parks of Oregon's Wallowa Mountains, and mountain meadows in central Idaho framed by dark huddles of subalpine fir. And though they may lack the sheer biomass of more westerly forests, there is much to be savored here. The silhouettes of curl-leaf mahoganies hanging from the lip of some high canyon can certainly reach out and grab you, in some ways as much as can the trunk of a mammoth western redcedar rising through a gray soup of coastal fog.

As you walk through these forests, you may enjoy examining the different vertical "layers" of such places. In much the same way that different life zones run up a mountain, offering birds and animals different niches to live in, so do the different canopy layers of a forest offer very different places for the residents to feed, nest, and even conduct their courtship rituals. In some cases this specialization becomes a rather fine art. In the coastal forests of Oregon and Washington, for example, the territories of the black-capped chickadee and chestnut-backed chickadee overlap. To settle the matter, the two birds have developed a rather sporting arrangement wherein the black-capped feeds in the lower portions of the tree and the chestnut-backed takes to the top. This is a fine example of how nature is less often a cutthroat struggle between species than it is an attempt to minimize such struggles by evolving specific, noncompetitive niches.

Something else to notice on these forest walks is that the tune plants dance to is by and large called by a blend of sunlight and moisture. A south-facing slope in Idaho's Pioneer Mountains will dry out much faster than will its north-facing counterpart, thus giving rise to a much different composition and density of plants. A young hemlock may slowly work its way up into the most shaded tree canopy, while its neighbor, the Douglas fir, won't be able to reproduce until there's enough of an opening in the canopy to let in sunlight. Such patterns are important clues to what's really going on in a forest—precious toeholds from which you can begin to see the real genius of natural design.

The Mountains

To lovers of mountains, the Northwest high country is like waking up on your seventh birthday to a banquet table lined with birthday cakes. The only real question is, where do you begin? These rocky folds and parapets are without question among the great mountains of the world. There are the towering, snowy reaches of Rainier and the dry yellow hills of the Seven Devils; the tortured wrinkles of the Coast Range and the long, high swells of the Lost River Range. You can have granite and you can have basalt, alpine meadows or ponderosa park lands, wet or dry, green or gray, in the absolute middle of nowhere or a mere stone's throw from the back side of the city.

No matter which Northwest range you happen to be talking about, these lands are for the most part so vast that it seems you can always manage to cut off a little slice just for yourself. Indeed, it was the incredible ruggedness of this land, a good share of it far too impenetrable for exploitation, that allowed much of the Northwest high country to remain in such pristine condition. Idaho, for example, most certainly would not be blessed with the 2.3-million-acre Frank Church–River of No Return Wilderness were it not for the fact that the region was too twisted and remote to be used for other purposes.

For those who enjoy the more puzzling aspects of natural science, sorting out the geological events that created the Northwest high country can be a lifetime affair. Here were vast island arcs scraping against the edges of an ancient continent, and volcanoes tossing ash and lava bombs across a landscape already blackened by eruptions. The greatest known flood in the history of the world occurred here, and glaciers ground the mountains into what are arguably some of the most rugged alpine headwalls and cirque basins on the continent. In all, it is a dizzy spin of uplift and erosion, the crunch of tectonic plates and the grind of glacial ice—even, according to some geologists, a giant meteorite that crashed into the southeastern corner of Oregon, giving birth to the vast sweep of the Columbia Plateau. Of course, while piecing together such puzzles is fun for some, it's hardly a prerequisite for being able to come down off these peaks with a smile on your face. Indeed, perhaps you agree with Walt Whitman, who cautioned, "You must not know too much, or be too scientific about birds and trees and flowers; a certain free margin, and even vagueness ... helps your enjoyment of these things."

One simpler pattern that you may enjoy tracking across these mountain trails, however, centers on how much of what you encounter on the face of a mountain is related to elevation. The higher you go, the cooler it gets. And since cool air masses can't hold as much moisture as warm ones, when mountain ranges force them upward they begin to condense into clouds, often loosing their cargo on the high slopes in the form of rain or snow. This is precisely how the Cascades manage to snatch so much precious water from the inland Northwest. It's also how Mount Rainier—standing so incredibly tall against such moist coastal air—produces some of the snowiest conditions in the world. Increasing moisture and decreasing temperatures cause not only the trees to be different the higher you go, but also shrubs, ground covers, and wildflowers. And this, in turn, means that the birds, mammals, insects, and amphibians will change too.

So much of America has changed dramatically since Lewis and Clark first punched their way across the rugged folds of the Bitterroots and since Alexander Ross of the Hudson's Bay Company trudged up the Sawtooth Valley to the headwaters of the Salmon River. Then again, thankfully, much has remained the same.

> In such places standing alone on the mountaintop it is easy to realize that whatever special nests we make—leaves and moss like the marmots and birds, or tents and piled stone—we all dwell in a house of one room—the world with the firmament for its floor—and are sailing the celestial spaces without leaving any track.
>
> —*John Muir,*
> John of the Mountains

▪ WASHINGTON ▪

WASHINGTON
. . .

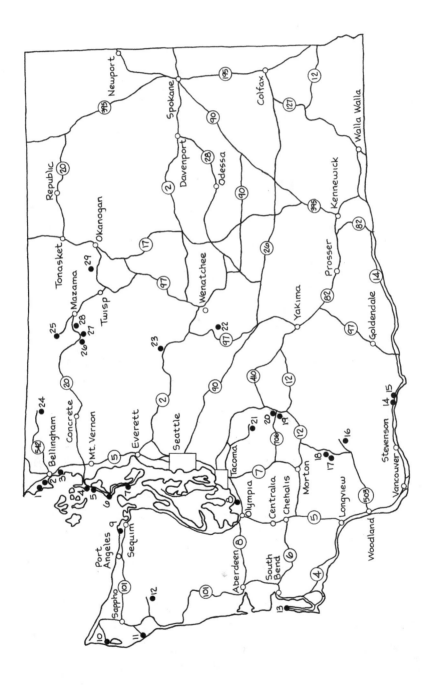

Western Washington

WALK #1—LAKE TERRELL WILDLIFE AREA

DISTANCE:	0.8 mile
ENVIRONMENT:	Forest
LOCATION:	From Interstate 5 north of Bellingham, take the Ferndale exit, and head west for 4.5 miles to Lake Terrell Road. Turn right. In 0.4 mile you'll see a small parking area at the south edge of Lake Terrell. Park here, and begin your walk on a dirt road that runs along the lakeshore.

Sandwiched between a grid of country farm roads, Lake Terrell isn't exactly a source of dramatic inspiration. Yet anyone who loves waterfowl—the quack of harlequin ducks or the white flash of whistling swans—will find this to be one of the more charming, and often uncrowded, nooks in all of northwest Washington. In fact, Lake Terrell currently plays host to every species of duck found in this portion of the state.

In the fall, Lake Terrell is the first stopover point for thousands of waterfowl heading south out of British Columbia along the Pacific Flyway. Although hunting is allowed during this time of year on about half of the reserve, an autumn visit can nonetheless be delightful. On any given day, 5,000 birds may drop out of the sky; as you'll see along the back side of our walk, refuge managers have planted corn and barley to help fuel the hungry fliers. (In one year, 4.5 tons of barley alone were planted over 60 acres.) Late each evening, well after the setting of the October sun, thousands of mallards, pintails, and Canada geese can be heard waddling into the surrounding fields to begin a night of feasting.

While winter, spring, and summer may lack some of the magnitude of the migration parade, they're also fine times to visit.

Raccoon

Blue herons fish, and northern harriers sail over the fields and wetlands looking for mice or young birds. Raccoons scour the shoreline for frogs, grebes fast-step across the water trying like mad to become airborne, coots dive for dinner, and beaver build ever better dams. Speaking of beaver, a few years back refuge managers removed a dam here that was causing flooding problems. Not only did the incensed rodents rebuild a 3-foot-high and 10-foot-wide dam in a single night, but this time wove it through with a thorny rose bush!

Our walk begins along a level dirt pathway, skirting a narrow corridor between the shore of Lake Terrell and a weave of alder, vine maple, blackberry, and pine. The small islands you see sticking out of the water were built to offer waterfowl nesting sites out of reach of hungry weasels and coyotes. Indeed, nesting is a time of extreme danger for most waterfowl, since it means leaving the safety of open water. Canada geese will sometimes take to high stumps for protection, while mallards have been known to nest in trees. Vulnerable western grebe chicks spend the first couple weeks of their lives on their parents' backs, riding in a special pouch located between the wing and back feathers. In this way, one parent can fish, while the youngsters bob around contentedly on the other one's back, far from the hungry jaws of a weasel or the talons of a northern harrier.

Stay along the lake shore for 0.45 mile, at which point you'll reach the paved entry road that leads to the refuge headquarters. Turn left here, and begin a quiet trek past a fine patchwork of vine maple, alder, and blackberries. (For a longer walk, you can take a right at the pavement and follow the road past the refuge headquarters and onto a dirt road that winds back to yet another Lake Terrell inlet.) You'll notice in places that the blackberries have grown into extremely dense thickets—wall after wall of fearsome thorns and barbs. Blackberries provide birds and other careful pickers with delicious fruit, and people have long used the berries, roots, and leaves of the blackberry to stop diarrhea. What's more, to this day herbalists still prescribe chewing the leaves of the plant as a treatment for bleeding gums.

All too soon—at 0.8 mile, to be exact—you'll find yourself back at your car. On most days, once around this loop is simply not enough. Head down the path yet again and see what all you missed the first time—that little marsh wren scurrying around a huddle of cattails, the fresh tracks of a black-tailed deer in the trailside mud, the trumpeter swan floating on the far side of the lake like a tiny puff of cloud.

WALK #2—TENNANT LAKE

DISTANCE: 0.5 mile
ENVIRONMENT: Forest
LOCATION: From Interstate 5 north of Bellingham, take exit 262, and head west for 0.5 mile to Hovander Road. Turn left (south). In 0.2 mile turn right onto Nielson Avenue, and follow this for 0.75 mile to the Tennant Lake Interpretive Center parking area. Our walk begins near the interpretive center, beside the large wooden observation tower.

Like Lake Terrell Wildlife Management Area just to the west, Tennant Lake is a bird-lover's dream. Besides an excellent wetland habitat, here you'll have the added delights of an herb garden you can actually touch, as well as a fine interpretive center (open Wednesday through Sunday).

The beginning of this trail is framed by a fine patch of cattails, a plant that for centuries has had tremendous value to people around the world. As a food source it is almost unparalleled. The roots can be roasted, the pollen used for flour, the flowers eaten like corn on the cob, and the young shoots eaten raw. Furthermore, the fuzzy down that covers the spikes in the fall was often collected by Northwest mountain men and stuffed into their shoes as an insulator against the cold. Native peoples used that same down as a chafeless diaper wrapping (rather as we use baby powder today), while elsewhere it was considered the perfect stuffing for pillows. Even the leaves were useful; women of various Native American cultures used them to weave mats that would then serve as flooring in lodges or sweat houses.

While cattails produce an impressive amount of seed (sometimes a quarter-million on a single spike), they're also adept at creating new plants by sending shoots up from horizontal stems. As you walk past these cattail marshes, keep your eyes open for dome-shaped structures made of mud and pieces of various plants. These are the homes of muskrats—creatures who have their own affinity for cattail, preferring to dine on the fleshy underwater stems. This is also a good place to see both marsh wrens and red-winged blackbirds.

The scene from the boardwalk is a wonderful watercolor of wigeons, shovelers, scaups, and teals bobbing on Tennant Lake; on clear days Mount Baker adds a splash of the dramatic, shimmering in the eastern sky. Look for red-tailed hawks scanning the surrounding fields for mice, or catch a glimpse of a northern harrier patrolling a patch of reeds for unsuspecting young birds. Whether you know much about how ecosystems work or not, if you sit on this preserve and watch for a while you can almost feel the interconnectedness between species—the interplay of plant and bird, the dance of predator and prey.

Trying to get a handle on which bird is which can be an overwhelming task. One thing that can make it easier is to think in terms of habitats. When it comes to feeding, for example, most of the birds here have certain places where they like to look for food. Marsh wrens spend their time hunting insects in thick, low marsh vegetation; in fact, they are the only wrens to be found in such places. Northern

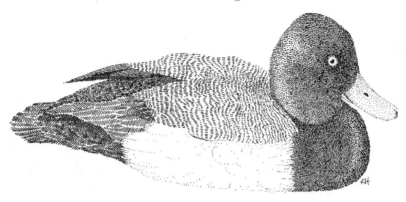

Lesser Scaup

shovelers, on the other hand, float in shallow places, straining water through their broad "shovel-like" bills. Ruddy ducks are deep-water divers; you'll need your binoculars to recognize them bobbing out in the middle of the lake. Both great blue and green herons wade in shallow water or stand on the edge of a bank, ever on the lookout for a fish to gobble. Indeed, the creatures who live here are not in a flurry of competition for the same food source; most have evolved as specialists, each able to capitalize on what's available in a particular niche of the environment.

In 0.1 mile the boardwalk splits. If you stay to the left, soon you'll come to a fine observation platform—the perfect place from which to survey this rich braid of marsh and open-water environments.

WALK #3—FRAGRANCE LAKE

DISTANCE: 2.2 miles
ENVIRONMENT: Forest
LOCATION: Larrabee State Park. From Interstate 5 south
of Bellingham, take exit 250, following the
signs for State Highway 11. Just north of
milepost 16, turn east on Highline Road. In
0.25 mile this road turns to gravel, and the
name changes to Fred Cleator Road. Follow
this route for 2.25 miles to the trailhead for
Fragrance Lake.

With a mix of cedar, salt air, and wild rose drifting up the lush hillsides that flank Samish Bay, Fragrance Lake definitely lives up to its name. Established in 1915, this is Washington's very first state park, and a fine preserve it is. The loop path around this lake is a perfect trek for slow-goers—those who can appreciate a leisurely rubbing of noses with sword ferns, cedar, broadleaf maple, and fir, as well as with fine seasonal eruptions of trillium, bleeding heart, currant, columbine, skunk cabbage, and calypso orchids.

From the trailhead you'll walk 0.6 mile along an old road grade to a parking area at the terminus of Fragrance Lake Road, which is now closed to public traffic. From this parking area follow the trail descending to the north, and in just 0.2 mile you'll meet the path coming to Fragrance Lake from State Highway 11. Turn right at this intersection, and soon you'll pass a beautiful patch of salal, growing thick and leathery along the right side of the trail. If you've not seen this common plant in the wild before, you may at least recognize its leaf from a delivery made to you by your local flower shop. The rich, hearty salal leaf is often used in commercial flower arrangements, tending to hold up well long after it's been cut. For people who lived in this region long ago, salal had a distinctly more pragmatic value. Besides eating the fruits, they often chewed or pounded salal leaves to treat painful burns or skin abrasions. Some Indian tribes also made a tea from the leaves, claiming that it relieved sore throats and coughs.

As you make your way along the south side of the lake, keep your eyes open for the belted kingfisher, which is sometimes seen perched

Belted Kingfisher

on shoreline branches or stumps, carefully scanning the water for dinner. It's a thrilling sight to see one of these solitary birds suddenly drop off its waterside perch and splash into the water, a second later flying back out with a small fish in its beak. The belted kingfisher's species name—*alcyone*—comes from Greek mythology. One day beautiful Alcyone was told that her seafaring husband had been killed in a shipwreck. Consumed by despair, Alcyone jumped into the ocean to end it all, but was instead changed into a kingfisher. The kingfisher is easily recognized by a white belt around the neck, and a tasseled tuft of head feathers that looks much the way some people's hair does when they first get out of bed in the morning.

As you round the back (north) side of the lake, on moist ground you may notice patches of a large-leaved plant sporting greenish spikes surrounded by a tall yellow bract open on one side. This is skunk cabbage, and if you happen to be close enough to smell the flowers, you'll understand where it got its name. While such odor may not be perfume to our noses, it's more than a little appealing to flies, which happen to be the plant's primary pollinators. (Generally, the flowers bloom too early to be pollinated by bees.) Like salal leaves, the leaves of skunk cabbage were often used to treat cuts and skin abrasions. The roots, however, were the main source of medicine, employed for everything from bronchial infections to venereal disease, asthma, and contraception.

Along the final quarter of your circle around Fragrance Lake, the path is framed by beautiful, sheer, sandstone cliffs, rising 50 to 60 feet through the forest canopy. Fragrance Lake lies in a tilted trough called a "plunging syncline." When glaciers poured through this ravine during the last ice age, they scooped out the softest rock, and thereby formed the basin for the lake. The ice also ground away at the walls of the ravine, leaving the cliffs of scoured, fairly erosion-resistant sandstone you see today. Glaciers form, by the way, not so much under conditions of bitter cold, but after an extended period of more snow falling in the cold season than is melting in the warm. After many years, these heavy layers compact into glacial ice.

WALK #4—ROSARIO BEACH

DISTANCE:	0.7 mile
ENVIRONMENT:	Coast
LOCATION:	Deception Pass State Park. From Interstate 5, head west on State Highway 20 for 16 miles. Turn right (north) following the signs for Rosario Beach. The trailhead is 1.2 miles down this road, adjacent to a picnic area. Our walk takes off from the west side of the turnaround loop, descending a small bluff onto a rocky beach filled with driftwood. (The main pathway—not ours—goes south, toward the large story totem near the picnic area.)

Rosario, which takes its name from the patroness of the Spanish exploring ship San Carlos, is a wonderful mix of rough, rocky headlands and shimmering tidal pools. Of course, if you'd like to explore the tidal pools, you should plan your visit for low tide. (The Deception Pass State Park office can tell you when low tide will occur.) Also, if you're new to the fine art of exploring tidal pools, be sure to take a guidebook to help you key out the various creatures you find there. If you end up arriving at high tide, you may want to investigate a longer, somewhat more rugged trail that takes off near the picnic grounds, heading east toward Bowman Bay and Lighthouse Point. This latter path will offer beautiful views, as well as a fine weave of plant life, including paintbrush, broom-rape, camas lily, stonecrop, kinnikinnick, and rice-root.

Upon first reaching the beach, make your way south past the large piles of driftwood toward a series of smooth, black tiers of basalt, each riddled with pockets of seawater. If you've never visited a tide pool area like this before, some of the first creatures you may want to take a look at are the barnacles that lie plastered to the rocks. Barnacles feed only when submerged in water, extending a small, feathery appendage known as a *cirri* to collect algae, microscopic animals, and the tiny eggs of other creatures.

Because barnacles always "eat in," they expend no energy trying to find food. Thus, their problem is not one of travel, but rather of how to stay put—in other words, how to keep from being ripped from their moorings by the strong slap of ocean waves. To achieve this, barnacles secrete an incredibly strong adhesive from glands located near their front pair of antennae. This cement is so powerful that corporate chemists spent years studying it in order to come up with their own formulas for super industrial adhesives. For a long time people didn't know what to think of this strange little critter with the calcium plates. Was it plant or was it animal? At one point, it was even suggested that barnacles were neither— that they in fact grew from seabird feathers that had dropped onto the rocks!

Something to remember if you happen to be looking for specific forms of sea life is that most creatures here are rather picky about how much time—if any—they spend either out of water or exposed to sunlight. An acorn barnacle or an eroded periwinkle can feed, rid itself of waste, and perform necessary respiration functions with relatively brief ocean dousings. Other plants and animals, such as bull kelp, starfish, and mussels, require much greater exposure to the ocean, and thus will be found farther down, in what are called—from highest to lowest—the middle littoral, lower littoral, and sublittoral zones. While setting up shop in such tight, specific zones might seem like a precarious way to live, in some ways it's not all that different from what terrestrial animals do. Many birds, mammals, reptiles, and insects live in life zones of their own, each one bracketed by a rather specific set of temperature and moisture requirements.

As you make your way out of the barnacle zone, watch for sea lettuce and the inflated bladders of rockweed, as well as sea urchins, chitons, feather dusters (actually a type of worm), purple shore crabs, and flat porcelain crabs. Before you leave the tide pools, one word of caution. As I've suggested, many of these creatures are extremely sensitive to changes in sunlight or moisture. Therefore, it's important during your explorations to not make drastic changes to their environment. If you pick up a rock to look for a crab, for instance, be sure to put it back just as you found it. Also, don't forget to glance occasionally toward open water. Besides spotting sea otters, you're likely to see western grebes, glaucous-winged gulls, osprey, double-crested and pelagic cormorants, and perhaps even a bald eagle or two.

When you're ready to head back, carefully make your way eastward up the headland to a small footpath. Take a right here, and you'll be on your way to a quick circle tour of Rosario Head, coming back out to the picnic area near the large totem in less than 0.3 mile. To the south you'll have fine views of North Beach on Whidbey Island, and to the southwest, the large, rocky promontory of Lighthouse Point.

Great Horned Owl

WALK #5—NORTH BEACH

DISTANCE: 2 miles

ENVIRONMENT: Coast

LOCATION: Deception Pass State Park. From Interstate 5 north of Mount Vernon, take exit 230 and head west on State Highway 20 for approximately 17.5 miles. Once you cross the bridge to Whidbey Island, turn right toward Deception Pass State Park Headquarters, and follow the signs to West Point in the West Beach parking area. Our walk heads east from this point, taking off from beneath a large totem that stands near the West Beach parking area.

There's a certain historical intrigue hanging on the cool salt air of Deception Pass—a wonderful mix of totem cultures and sailing ships and fishermen homesteaders. Indeed, your first steps along this trail will pass by a beautiful bear totem—a replica of one used by the Haida, who centered north of here, in the Queen Charlotte Islands. As indicated on the interpretive sign, the Haida sometimes came south into the Whidbey Island area to take slaves. But that isn't the only reason they left home; Haida were considered to be the most widely traveled of all the region's native residents, making regular forays in all directions to trade, fish, and hunt.

Outside of doctors and shamans, there were three classes of people in Haida society: chiefs, noblemen, and commoners. Slaves, as you might expect, were at the beck and call of those in the upper tiers. As horrible a fate as being taken a slave would have been, one could have done worse than to have been carted off by the Haida. Haida slaves were rarely beaten or tortured in the course of daily life, as they were in many other cultures, including our own. What's more, Haida captives were usually allowed to marry and have their own families, and many were later ransomed and taken back home by their relatives.

Though the Haida ate a wide variety of seafood, they made a staple out of salmon taken from coastal streams and rivers with spears, dam-traps, and dip nets. For countless years the Haida lived in relative harmony with the land, their populations balanced with the abundance of natural resources. In the end, though, they fared poorly under the advance of the Europeans. In the mid-1850s the Haida numbered about 8,000; by 1895, fewer than 600 remained.

Our trail begins by climbing a small rock promontory flush with tall Oregon grape, salal, and salmonberry—all of which were food sources for the Haida and other coastal cultures. In 0.1 mile the path drops into the park amphitheater, where you may have trouble finding it again. The easiest route is to head for the northeast corner of the amphitheater parking lot—in other words, the corner closest to the beach and to the Deception Pass Bridge. Beyond this parking area the trail generally parallels the beach though a cool green forest of Douglas fir and cedar, with occasional smatterings of lodgepole (shore pine), red alder, and madrone.

If ever you were to pick a spot to watch the dynamics of tides, this stretch of Deception Pass would be the place. Tides result from the gravitational relationship that exists between the earth, moon, and to a lesser degree, the sun. The moon affects a fairly strong draw on the earth, actually pulling the oceans upward and then releasing them again each time it circles the earth. (Of course it also pulls on the land, but since the land is much denser, there is little response.) We can predict this pulling (high tide) and this releasing (low tide) because we know precisely how long the moon's journey takes. But you may wonder why, when the moon orbits the earth only once in a 24-hour period, there are two high tides and two low tides each day. As it turns out, when the moon tugs at the earth, it has little effect on the oceans lying on the opposite side of the planet. In fact, centrifugal force makes them bulge away from the earth, though to a lesser degree, thus causing another high tide. Low tides, then, can be thought of as simply marking the halfway point of two simultaneously occurring high tides.

As for the role of the sun, on the two days each month that it aligns with the moon and earth, the additional gravitational draw leads to a very high tide, known as a spring tide. On the two days each month that the sun is at right angles to the moon, we have very low tides, or "neap tides."

Funneled through this narrow passageway, the tidal flows at Deception Pass are especially dramatic—a roiling river of seawater

Peregrine Falcon

charging alternately east or west at a fierce pace. On a strong ebb tide, 2.5 billion gallons of water boil through the narrowest part of the channel every hour. Obviously, the combination of fast water in a narrow channel sets up some rather perilous conditions for navigators. Canoe Pass, which is the smaller of the two channels underneath the bridge you see ahead, was so named by pioneers because nothing much larger than a canoe could safely negotiate it.

The many side trails off the main North Beach path can be confusing; basically, just keep heading east toward the Deception Pass Bridge, paralleling the beach whenever possible. In 1 mile the trail will enter a large beachside picnic area. This is an idyllic spot, carved out of a magnificent forest of Douglas fir, cedar, and Sitka spruce—the trunks rising from an airy, almost ethereal understory of sword fern. From this point follow the pathway down to the beach, and if the tide is low enough, plan to return to West Point via the beach. In winter this is a fine place to look for bald eagles, who dine regularly on salmon, as well as on a ducklike bird known as the western grebe. If you're here in March, check out the cliffs on your left for brilliant sprays of red-flower currant. Just about the time that coastal residents are suffering from terminal cases of winter green-and-gray, the red-flower currant bursts on the scene and literally shouts "spring!" It's one of the first blooms to appear, and it would be hard to imagine a more beautiful beginning to the season.

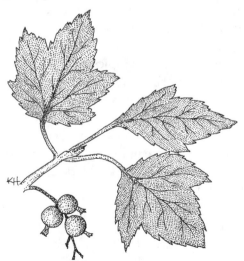

Red-flower Currant

WALK #6—POINT PARTRIDGE

DISTANCE: 2 miles

ENVIRONMENT: Coast

LOCATION: Fort Ebey State Park. From the Deception Pass Bridge at the northern edge of Whidbey Island, head south on State Highway 20 for about 16 miles, and turn right (west), following the signs for Fort Ebey State Park. Once in the park, you'll come to a "T" intersection. Turn left, and follow the signs to the old gun battery emplacement. Our trail takes off near a picnic area, on the north side of a high bluff overlooking the Strait of Juan de Fuca.

Believe me, the deep, fresh beauty of this Whidbey Island coastline will grab you long before you take your first steps north on the trail to Point Partridge. From the trailhead on a clear day you can look across the blue waters of the Strait of Juan de Fuca to the bold faces of the Olympic Mountains, rising from the breast of the Olympic Peninsula like the gates of a strange and haunting spirit world. Indeed, in coastal Indian mythology these mountains were the source of many mysteries—from the fierce mountain monster Tacobud, who swallowed those who came to the high country searching for game and wild berries, to the beautiful Valley of Peace, a place high in the Olympics where once each year all nations could put down their war clubs and come together in harmony. Rather at odds with this latter vision of peace was the creation of Fort Ebey itself, built during World War II and outfitted with two 6-inch guns for use against any enemy ships that might stray too close to the entrance of Puget Sound. While the guns are gone, you can still walk through the dark concrete fortification tunnels, located at the south end of the picnic area.

This park takes its name from an early pioneer by the name of Colonel Issac Ebey. Ebey served for a time as a customs collector for the government, and in 1850 established a rather thriving commercial area known as Ebey's Landing, located just to the south. As good as life on Whidbey Island was to Colonel Ebey, his death was particularly tragic. On a warm summer night in 1857, a Kake tribe of Haida Indians climbed in their canoes and headed south out of the Queen Charlotte Islands, each bent on dishing out some serious payback for a battle fought with U.S. troops near Port Gamble the previous autumn. During that skirmish 27 Indians were killed, one of whom was a chief. Determined to even the score—one chief for another—the warriors made their way onto Colonel Ebey's farm on the night of August 11, shot him, and then fled back to Canada with his head in their hands. It was only through the extraordinary efforts of one of Colonel Ebey's friends, a steamship captain named Charles Dodd, that three years later the head was returned and buried with the body in Sunnyside Cemetery, overlooking nearby Ebey's Landing.

The beginning of our walk passes through a fine coastal mix of salal, Douglas fir, ocean spray, red-flower currant, and an occasional rhododendron. If you're here from late April through June, you'll also see clusters of yellow pealike flowers growing on a shrub with stiff green twigs. This is broom, and although not a native, it's one of the most common plants in all of western Washington. Broom takes its name from the fact that during the Middle Ages it really was used as a broom (though never when flowers were on the plant, since to do so was to flirt with bad luck). Though the upper portions of the broom plant contain toxins, during the 1500s and 1600s broom was commonly used as a diuretic and a laxative.

In 0.2 mile you'll see the smooth, terra-cotta–colored bark of a Pacific madrone tree on the right side of the path. This is one of

Ocean Spray

• 19 •

Yellow-rumped Warbler

the most beautiful of all the trees in the Pacific West. Just as the bark catches your eye even in a crowded forest, peeling away in strips during midsummer to reveal bright green layers of inner bark underneath, so too do old leaves add their share of color, bunches of them turning a burnt scarlet before dropping to the forest floor. As if all that weren't enough, from March to May the madrone also sports lovely cream-colored, bell-shaped flowers, which eventually yield to yellow or orange fruits. A short distance past this Pacific madrone are nice clusters of ocean spray, their foamy-looking, ivory flowers adding yet another shade of beauty to this high coastal ledge.

Perhaps as noticeable as the plants you do see along this path are the plants you don't. While nearby Seattle receives about 36 inches of rain annually, this portion of Whidbey Island comes in with a rather meager 18 inches. Coastal plants that require more moisture are either absent or else grow only in protected ravines.

Soon the trail begins a fairly gradual descent to ocean level, at 0.5 mile passing a quiet little hollow brimming with hemlocks, sword fern, and salal. Besides the occasional songs of the red-breasted nuthatch, western tanager, yellow-rumped warbler, western pewee, or pine sisken, the only other sound is the slow, rich rhythm of ocean waves, the song softened a bit by the small hill lying just to the west. The quiet reserve of this little woodland is broken rather suddenly in another 0.1 mile, as the trail breaks out onto a precipice teetering 200 feet above a narrow ribbon of rocky beach. Notice the misshapened Douglas fir and hemlock trees growing on this exposed location, most sporting branches only on one side. This kind of growth is sometimes called "flagging," and it's a result of the pruning accomplished by the winter winds that come roaring across this open ledge. Similar, but even more dramatic flagging can be seen on trees that grow along the exposed highlands of the Cascade or the Olympic mountains.

From here the pathway continues to descend past some lovely wild rose bushes, finally reaching the Point Partridge picnic area, at sea level, in 0.9 mile. It's a short walk to the beach—a rather cobbly place littered with intriguing collections of driftwood.

You'll be interested to know that Fort Ebey State Park is part of the nation's first national historical reserve, established in 1978. Known as Ebey's Landing National Historic Reserve, this is an unusual mix of private lands (which make up 90 percent of the reserve), as well as town, county, and state parks. The 17,000-acre complex is managed as a unit of the National Park Service. The reserve was created with support from local residents, who strongly agreed with the official intent of "preserving a rural community which provides an unbroken historic record from the 19th-century exploration and settlement in Puget Sound to the present time." While you're in the area, you may also want to visit historic Coupeville and the Admiralty Head Lighthouse, as well as do a bit more walking at either Ebey's Landing or Fort Casey State Park.

Wild Rose

WALK #7—WILBERT TRAIL

DISTANCE:	1.2 miles
ENVIRONMENT:	Forest
LOCATION:	South Whidbey State Park. From the junction of state highways 20 and 525 on Whidbey Island, head south on Highway 525 for 4.5 miles, and turn right (west) onto Smugglers Cove Road. Our trailhead is 4 miles down this road, on the left; the main entrance to South Whidbey State Park is 0.4 mile farther, on the right. (Coming from the south, the turnoff to Smugglers Cove is about 17 miles north of the ferry dock.)

Hear the voice of the Bard!
Who Present, Past, and Future sees,
Whose ears have heard
The Holy Word
That walked among the ancient trees.
                                        —*William Blake*

With the recent controversy over the survival of the spotted owl, few people in America aren't at least casually aware of the old growth forests of the Pacific Northwest. Truly, these are environments like none other on earth. Beyond their almost haunting beauty, it is a remarkable experience to amble among trees that are 300, 500, or even 1,000 years old. Wedged between the feet of these giants is a window into what seems an altogether different reality—an unfolding of time that is so far outside of our typical day-to-day experience as to leave us nearly intoxicated, spinning in the rhythms of forever.

A Pacific Northwest old growth forest requires about 200 years to develop; most, like this one, are more in the neighborhood of 300 to 500 years old. As you'll see when you walk the Wilbert Trail, the number of plants growing on the floor of such forests depends on how much light makes it past the layers of needles that tower high overhead. In some places the canopy is so thick that the ground is nearly bare. When a big tree does fall, however, it's almost as if a starting gun has been fired; over the years that follow,

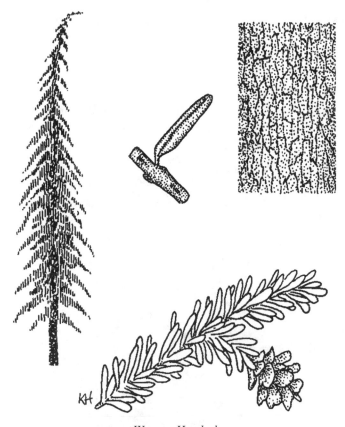

Western Hemlock

a variety of shrubs and wildflowers can be seen jockeying for a place in the sun. Likewise, a young hemlock that may have been waiting patiently in deep shade for 20 years will experience remarkable growth when the forest canopy finally opens.

This preserve was once referred to as a "Classic U Forest." For years the state of Washington had sold the timber from its forested lands, with the money going to support the University of Washington; hence, the "U" stood for "university." This tract of land was slated for just such a harvest when a group of local people, headed by a retired engineer named Harry Wilbert, began a vigorous effort to save it. Thankfully, the group was successful. In 1993 the forest was brought under the protection of South Whidbey State Park.

As you make your way around this loop, take a close look at some of the plants that seem to be thriving in the shaded areas.

Notice how many sport fairly good-sized leaves with few or no hairs on them, giving them a smooth luster. This is no accident. Both size and hairlessness help these plants maximize their ability to conduct photosynthesis under low light conditions.

A short distance into the walk is an intersection. Follow the right fork, signed "Ancient Cedar," and soon you'll find yourself at the feet of a magnificent, 500-year-old western redcedar. It's a rather humbling thought to consider that when this tree was a young seedling, Leonardo da Vinci was just putting the finishing touches on the Mona Lisa. Most of the other trees you'll see along the trail—many of them Douglas firs—range in age from 200 to 300 years.

Coltsfoot

Headed down the main trail again, you'll meander through groves of Douglas fir, western hemlock, and, in the wetter areas, Sitka spruce; in addition, there are some fine groves of red alder visible through the forest on your left. Notice how the large conifers of the forest have few or no branches along the lower portions of their trunks. Trees that grow close together often "self-prune." They do this because so little sun comes in that these lower branches can hardly earn their keep when it comes to producing energy. Very large conifers may not have a single branch growing along the first hundred feet of their trunks.

Take a right at the "T" intersection at 0.2 mile, where you'll see some nice tufts of Oregon grape, twinflower, and red huckleberry. Shortly after this junction is a fallen Douglas fir, which is now serving as a "nurse log" to several small hemlocks. In very moist forests you can sometimes spot trees that have very distinct arches at the base of their trunks—often large enough for a person to crawl through. What likely happened is that for many years the tree straddled a nurse log like this one; when the nurse log finally decomposed—a process that may take centuries—the tree on top was left with an arched base, planted in the ground like a bow-legged cowboy.

Continue past a wet area stitched with a weave of skunk cabbage, deer fern, and various mosses—a kind of fairyland, guarded by the ancient trees. At 0.85 mile you'll reach an intersection with a service road. Turn right here, and follow the road for a hundred yards or so past beautiful thickets of salmonberry and patches of horsetail to the Smugglers Cove Highway. If you're here in early spring, scan the sides of the highway for coltsfoot blooms. These silky, purplish-white flowers are among the first of spring's flowers, sometimes opening up before the plant has even had a chance to unfurl its leaves.

WALK #8—BROWN FARM DIKE TRAIL

DISTANCE: 5.5 miles
ENVIRONMENT: Coast
LOCATION: Nisqually National Wildlife Refuge. From Interstate 5, 7 miles east of Olympia, turn off at exit 114, and follow the signs 0.5 mile to the Nisqually National Wildlife Refuge parking area. Maps of the refuge and additional interpretive information are located near the parking lot. Please note that this is a hiking trail only (no bikes allowed); also, pets are not permitted on the refuge. *Note:* The outer portion of the Brown Farm Dike Trail is closed during waterfowl hunting season, usually from mid- to late October through the 1st of January.

Though 5.5 miles may seem like a long trek, along the Brown Farm Dike Trail it will pass with the greatest of ease. One can hardly go a hundred yards along this trail without spotting something of interest: the deep scarlets of salmonberry blooms along the Nisqually River, or the flash of a northern flicker in a grove of cottonwoods; the splash of a river otter in McAllister Creek, or the grand swoop of a red-tailed hawk as it plucks a vole from the shaggy fields of Alson Brown's old farm. Indeed, on the back side of this loop nature almost seems to arrive in stereo—freshwater marshes on your left stitched with wrens, snipes, great blue herons, red-winged blackbirds, and bitterns; and the saltwater flats to your right sporting glaucous-winged gulls, sandpipers, wigeon, scoters, goldeneyes, and buffleheads.

Armed with little more than a horse-drawn plow-bucket, in 1904 Alson Brown began to turn this delta into productive farmland by building a system of dikes to hold back the seawater. When the farm finally petered out in the mid-1960s, the area came dangerously close to being turned into either a sanitary landfill or a site for a cargo port. The beauty you see here today is thanks primarily to Margaret McKenny and several local environmental and sporting groups, whose tireless efforts resulted in the establishment of the Nisqually National Wildlife Refuge in 1974. Remarkably, this

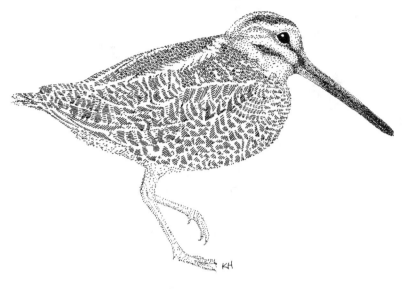

Common Snipe

refuge provides either a permanent or temporary home for a whopping 300 species of fish, birds, reptiles, mammals, and amphibians. In a single winter, up to 20,000 birds will find food and shelter here. If you'd like to feast your eyes and ears on the migration parade that passes through Nisqually, plan your visit from mid-March through mid-May, or from mid-September through early December. (Do, however, take note of seasonal closures.)

By the time you've walked 0.5 mile along the Brown Farm Dike Trail, the noisy bustle of Interstate 5 will for the most part have yielded to quiet patchworks of lowland marshes and fine weaves of cottonwood, bigleaf maple, and alder. Also scattered along much of the trail are patches of Indian plum. This shrub is one of the first plants to get down to business in the spring, its brilliant green leaves and fragile clusters of small white flowers lending a special beauty to an otherwise drab forest. Like another early bloomer that grows a little farther down the trail, the skunk cabbage, the flowers of Indian plum have a rather fetid odor. Though hardly an enticing smell to our noses, this skunky perfume is the perfect draw for the flies that will pollinate the plant.

A half-mile is also about the point where you'll join the lovely Nisqually River, which in various places is framed by patches of salmonberry. From here to the point where the path turns west is

Rufous-sided Towhee

Wilson's Warbler

Cedar Waxwing

a good stretch to watch (and listen!) for belted kingfishers, rufous-sided towhees, Wilson's and yellow-rumped warblers, cedar wax-wings, and song sparrows. If you enjoy birding, you may want to investigate the small 0.5 mile Ring Dike Loop, which takes off from the main trail at 1.2 miles into the walk.

An especially nice addition to the refuge, constructed for the Washington centennial in 1989, is a large wooden observation deck, located 2.2 miles into our walk. Jutting out into the fringes of the mud flats, this is a wonderful place to survey the Nisqually Reach portion of Puget Sound. In fall you can witness a marvelous clatter of bird life—herons, gulls, ducks, and geese, seemingly with no end.

Soon the trail takes a southward turn up the muddy tidal reaches of McAllister Creek. The abundance of blackberry and wild rose make this an ideal place to grab the bird books yet again. Continue to follow the small roadway south until it turns east, near an interpretive sign about the Medicine Creek Treaty of 1854, which granted fishing rights to native peoples of the region. You can still see Indian fishing nets in both McAllister Creek and the Nisqually River.

The Medicine Creek Treaty was engineered by the governor of the territory, Issac Stevens, who met with the Indians of the Tacoma and Olympia regions of Washington at a halfway point known as Medicine Creek. Originally, the politicians of the region wanted to create one large temporary reservation to hold the people of all tribes until each could be shipped to a remote patch of farmland faraway from settled territory. (At the time, many Americans believed that all native peoples, no matter where they lived, should be turned into farmers.)

In the end the natives wisely refused to let go of their traditional fishing areas, so instead, three small reservations were created. One of the most outrageous aspects of this entire treaty process was the fact that Governor Stevens required all negotiations to be conducted not in the tribe's own language, which he easily could have done, but in what was sometimes called "Chinook"—a kind of pidgin developed by early traders, consisting of no more than a few hundred words. Using this language would have made it impossible for even the basics of a treaty to be adequately defined. So common were these kinds of abuses that, two years later, one of the governor's own employees refused to go to battle against the Indians, claiming that political stupidity had caused the fighting in the first place.

Ten years after the Medicine Creek Treaty, a fellow named John Beeson began to voice strong objections to the deplorable treatment of the Indians in the Oregon Territory. When the Methodist Church announced that, as far as it was concerned, the Indians of the region were still "wretched heathens, in the lowest depths of moral degradation," Beeson was quick to respond. "Let them," he pleaded, "at least have a religion that will not insult their common sense by presenting itself with Whiskey and Creeds in one hand and Bibles and Bowie-knives in the other." Beeson was angrily attacked by his neighbors, and in the end forced to leave his farm in the middle of the night to escape being hung, or at least thoroughly beaten. He continued his fight for the native peoples of this region back in the East, and eventually even caught the ear of President Lincoln. "If we get through the war and I live,"

Lincoln is said to have told him, "this Indian system shall be reformed."

As you head back east along the last leg of our walk, notice the large crosslike structures on either side of the path. These are raptor perches. You're most likely to see either a red-tailed hawk or northern harrier sitting here, though visitors to the refuge on a cloudy winter day may also spot the short-eared owl—a bird that starts hunting for mice and small rodents long before it gets dark. Other birds sometimes seen on these perches include American kestrels and rough-legged, sharp-shinned, and Cooper's hawks.

Rough-legged Hawk

WALK #9—DUNGENESS SPIT

DISTANCE: 2 miles
ENVIRONMENT: Coast
LOCATION: Dungeness National Wildlife Refuge. From about 4 miles west of Sequim on U.S. Highway 101, turn north onto Kitchen-Dick Lane. (This will be about 1 mile west of mile marker 261.) Proceed for 3.35 miles to Voice of America Road, where you'll turn left. Follow this for 1.1 miles, passing through the Clallam County–Dungeness Recreation Area Campground, and finally into the large parking area for the Dungeness Spit Trail.

Dungeness Spit, which traces a gentle arc for 5.5 miles into the salty waters of the Strait of Juan de Fuca, is the stuff of which beach-walking dreams are made. On one side of you will be the gentle slap of surf against the sand, while on the other, across a rugged backbone of driftwood, is an estuary fed by the Dungeness River—a favorite resting place for thousands of birds, and a nursery for no less than five kinds of salmon. If you're in the mood to just walk and walk some more, to put your feet on automatic and make a deep dive into the rhythms of the wind and the waves, the Dungeness Spit is the place.

Reaching the sand spit itself requires a 0.5-mile trek through a fine woodland environment. Here you'll see nice stands of Douglas fir, cedar, alder, Pacific madrone, and grand fir, all underlain by patches of ocean spray, Oregon grape, false lily-of-the-valley, Indian plum, and bedstraw. Also growing near the beginning of our walk, though not easily visible from the trail, is a large manzanita bush. This beautiful shrub is a lover of dry lands, so its presence is testimony to the fact that much of the moisture that falls on the rest of the Washington Coast does not fall here; the nearby Olympic Mountains block most of the incoming storms, leaving Dungeness Spit with less than 18 inches of rain a year.

At 0.4 mile is an observation deck framed by red-flower currant and, on the back side, a nice pair of Douglas firs. Here you'll find not only some good interpretive information, but also splendid views of Dungeness Spit. This landform, like many others in the area, was named by the great Northwest coastal explorer Captain George Vancouver. He called it New Dungeness because it reminded him of another long spit of land in the British Channel, called simply "Dungeness." Nearly a century later, local pioneers referred to the arm of land that juts southward from the main spit by the rather unsettling name of Graveyard Spit. Supposedly, 30 natives were buried here—all massacred by the Clallam Indians in 1875.

Now that you have already passed through one of the Dungeness ecosystems—the coniferous forest—standing on this platform will give you good views of the refuge's other habitats. These include estuaries, where the freshwater of the Dungeness River mixes with seawater; tidal flats, where, depending on the time of year, you'll likely find scurrying dunlins, sanderlings, and the ever-wary black-bellied plover; the open ocean, which is the domain of whales, porpoises, and harbor seals; and finally, the spit itself, which is an important nesting area for various shorebirds. All in all, more than 250 species of birds have been recorded at this refuge. In winter the place is especially enchanting—thick with the flutter and squawk of grebes, red-throated loons, and literally thousands of black brant, surf scoters, American wigeon, buffleheads, and goldeneyes.

Once on the beach, you can stroll to your heart's content. Though the spit can be busy on weekends, the farther out you go, the more potent the mix of sea and solitude becomes. The one sad note to all of this is that the protected areas of Dungeness just aren't big enough to serve the rush of life that comes and goes from these waters with each roll of the seasons. Right now there are several proposals for development along the private sectors of the harbor, some of which could seriously affect wintering wildlife populations. There will never be another place like Dungeness—for us, or for the wild creatures it sustains. Let's hope that we have the wisdom to adequately protect it.

WALK #10—CAPE ALAVA

DISTANCE:	7 miles
ENVIRONMENT:	Coast
LOCATION:	Olympic National Park. From U.S. Highway 101 at the village of Sappho, turn north onto Burnt Mountain Road. In about 10 miles you'll join State Highway 112. Follow Highway 112 through the town of Clallam Bay, and then turn south onto the Hoko-Ozette Road, which is located 0.5 mile past mile marker 13. Take the Hoko-Ozette Road for about 21.5 miles, where it will dead-end at a parking area near our trailhead. Follow the signs for the Indian Village Nature Trail and Cape Alava. *Note:* Much of the trail is along a boardwalk that can be very slippery when wet; good tennis shoes are the best bet for safe passage.

Along the coastal portions of Olympic National Park, rugged headlands splay cold ocean waves, while in the distance, dark sea stacks and spruce-capped volcanic islands rise out of the sea like the parapets of Avalon. All in all, this slice of Washington has as many faces as there are variations in the weather. On any given day it can be sunny and smiling, somber and fog-bound, or filled with raging winter winds, driving waves hard against the rocks. In all its moods, however, this is a beautiful place—one of the last great untrammeled seashores in America. This particular trail was a favorite of former Supreme Court Justice and conservationist William O. Douglas, who called it a place of "deep solitude and haunting beauty."

First to greet you on this walk is a lush weave of forest, spiked with a sweet perfume of cedar and Sitka spruce. The more-than-100 inches of rain that fall here each year have created a surprising number of variations on the theme of green. There's the leathery green of salal and the soft green of licorice fern, sword fern, and Pacific ewe; there's the fresh green of spring salmonberry and huckleberry leaves, and the dark, rich greens of hemlocks and spruces. As you might imagine, the trees and plants that thrive here are those with a high tolerance for shade. In a forest undisturbed by fire, wind, or disease, shade-tolerant cedars and hemlocks will sooner or later overtake sun-loving broadleaf trees, leaving the latter to work life out on the edges of streams, roads, and other clearings.

As you make your way toward Cape Alava, notice the difference in water clarity in some of the small streams you pass. Some flow crystal clear, while others run rusty. This coppery color is organic debris, and it's especially evident where catch pools have been created by logs falling across the watercourse. These pools also offer a habitat for several kinds of fish and insects that wouldn't be able to thrive in fast-flowing water.

At 0.1 mile you'll come to a split in the trail. Stay to the right here, following the signs for Cape Alava. If you're up for a hardy walk during low tide, you could hit Cape Alava, make your way south for about 3 miles along the beach to Sand Point, and then return on the trail you see coming in from the left. The total distance for such a walk is a hefty 10 miles; and yet those would be 10 of the most beautiful miles you could ever hope to set foot on. Roughly 2 miles past this trail junction you'll come to a large clearing. This is a remnant of Lars Ahlstrom's homestead, which was the western-most homestead in the continental United States. Ahlstrom came here in 1902 and stayed for 56 years, before a severe foot infection finally forced him to leave. Look for patches of swamp laurel here, its flowers lending beautiful splashes of reddish-pink. If you look closely at swamp laurel flowers, you'll see that some of the anther stalks are curved backward, the tips held by the base of the petals. Insects landing on these "triggers" cause the anther to spring upward, which lets loose a shower of pollen.

At 3.4 miles, just after passing through a patch of skunk cabbage, you'll near the shore of beautiful Cape Alava; from here, your entryway to the coast will be across a beautiful grassy park, studded with Sitka spruce and scouler willow. This is a wonderful place to spot black-tailed deer, some of them so tame that you may think you took a wrong turn and ended up at the local petting zoo. Don't get too fresh with these animals, however; if a black-tailed deer feels threatened, it can land a hard strike with its front hooves.

Hopefully, you've allowed plenty of time for exploring this beach. If it's low tide, take a look at potholes in the shore rocks for acorn barnacles, plate limpets, hermit crabs, sea urchins, roundworms, anemones, sea spiders, and rock whelks, as well as sea moss and sea tar, the latter which does indeed look like a patch of tar. This coastline is also a good place to spot some rather exotic birds. There's the rhinoceros auklet, which during breeding lets out a moan that sounds rather like a teenage cow whose voice has yet to break. Also here is the beautiful tufted puffin, with its orange, parrotlike bill, the rather solitary pigeon guillemot, and the common murre, whose offspring begin adolescence by making dramatic, 40-foot leaps into the sea from their ledgetop nests.

The "Indian Village" that you saw signs for when you were first starting this walk refers to a village that archaeologists excavated just to the north of here—one of the most significant on the Northwest coast. From what researchers can piece together, one night around 1500 or 1600 a great mud slide engulfed a town of Makah Indians while they slept, sealing the people and their many possessions into a time capsule, much the way that volcanic ash has preserved communities in other regions of the world. The finds here have been spectacular. They include intricate decorated baskets and cedar boxes, blankets made from a now-extinct "wool-producing" dog, ceremonial clubs, whale harpoons, and a sculpture of a whale's fin inlaid with hundreds of sea otter teeth that are in the shape of a thunderbird.

An even more amazing discovery at the Cape Alava dig were pieces of metal completely different from those being made in Spain, Russia, or Great Britain—the only European countries that could have possibly been trading with the Makah at the time. (Sir Francis Drake is thought to have passed this area on a voyage he made in 1579.) Based on these bits of metal, researchers now think that the Makah were trading not with Europeans, but with Asians! The metal was perhaps carried across the Bering Strait by Eskimos, down through the Aleutian Islands, and eventually into the intricate trade system of the Northwest, which generally ranged from northern California to Alaska.

While you're sitting here on this rugged, wind-torn coastline, it's easy to fantasize about early explorers drifting by in their wooden ships, the crew peering past the sea stacks into the dark, forested flanks of the Olympics. One of these early sailors, Captain James Cook, happened to trade some pieces of metal with the local Indians for otter skins that the crew needed for bedding. When Cook later sailed to China he was astounded to find that

the Chinese were willing to offer the equivalent of a year's salary—
$50 to $100—for a single otter pelt! Heavy trading, however,
was still a few years off, stymied by wars raging in both Europe and
the United States. When it did get going, though, it got going in a
big way.

American trading ships typically came out of Boston, and
needed almost a full year to make the trip around Cape Horn, out
to the Hawaiian Islands for provisioning, and then finally to the
Northwest coast. Once loaded with pelts, the ships sailed for
China, where the furs were traded for spices, tea, and sometimes
silver. Ships would then typically head back to Boston, making port
there two and a half to three years after their initial departure.
Though at first profits were very high, this kind of commerce
wasn't without serious cost. Before long every sailor and his uncle
were getting into the skin game; by 1820, the bulk of the Northwest
sea otter population had been wiped out.

WALK #11—SECOND BEACH

DISTANCE: 1.4 miles
ENVIRONMENT: Coast
LOCATION: Olympic National Park. From the town of
Forks, head north on U.S. Highway 101.
Drive 0.1 mile past mile marker 193, and
turn left (west). In 7.8 miles you'll reach a
fork in the road; stay left, and continue for
5.1 more miles. The trailhead for Second
Beach will be on the left side of the road.

If you've had about all of Highway 101 you can stand, by all
means make the 13-mile drive to Second Beach, where, after a walk
of just 0.7 mile, you'll find yourself on a stunning stretch of
seacoast. I arrived here on a still afternoon, with just a touch of gray
in the air; at first I thought I'd passed through some kind of
geography warp, landing on some wild, rock-strewn coast of Den-
mark. This isn't merely the ocean, but the sea. Like some of the old
growth forests that still flank a few of the region's river bottoms,
Second Beach has a timeless, ponderous feeling to it. This was
Shakespeare's kind of coast, "bound in with the triumphant sea,
whose rocky shore beats back the envious siege of watery Neptune."

As you begin your walk, look to the right of the path for a nice
patch of false lily-of-the-valley; during May, rising above patches
of shiny, heart-shaped leaves will be spikes of cream-colored
flowers. Opposite this little garden, on the other side of the trail,
look for a large conifer that appears to be standing on stilts. This
kind of growth occurs when a tree takes root on top of a log or
stump. When the "nurse log" or stump finally rots away—a process
that may take hundreds of years—the new tree is left looking like
this one.

Continue past groves of Sitka spruce, western hemlock,
cedar, and red alder, underlain by a mix of salal, salmonberry,
skunk cabbage, sword fern, and deer fern. Shortly after you begin
descending a series of wooden steps at 0.5 mile, you'll see a lush
ravine on the right side of the trail. This is an especially good place
to look for trillium—a plant with three large, deeply veined leaves
and, from mid-April through May, a beautiful white or sometimes

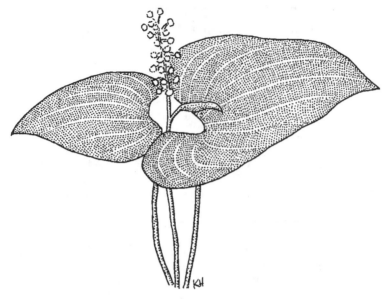

False Lily-of-the-Valley

pinkish flower. Trillium is still sometimes referred to as "birthroot," a name that stems from its use by Indians and some pioneers to stop bleeding after childbirth. This plant has also had several magical properties attributed to it, including use as a love potion.

At the bottom of the stairs you'll find yourself standing at the edge of a wonderful world of wind and waves and sea stacks. To your right lies a splendid "blowhole," where surging seawater shoots through an opening in the volcanic rock. Not surprisingly, early mariners considered the coastline from here to Cape Flattery, about 35 miles to the north, to be one of the most dangerous on the entire Pacific coast. During the early days of fur trading many ships were ground to splinters as they tried to make their way to the mouth of the Quillayute River, just north of where you now stand.

At the time, this shore was still home to the Quillayute Indians. Historians believe that the Quillayute would sometimes use these high, rugged offshore islands as fortresses, rolling rocks down on anyone either brave or stupid enough to pursue them.

WALK #12—SOUTH FORK HOH RIVER

DISTANCE: 3.6 miles
ENVIRONMENT: Forest
LOCATION: Olympic National Park and the Washington State Department of Natural Resources. From the town of Forks, head south on U.S. Highway 101, and turn right left (east) on a road that takes off at mile marker 176. (This turn is about a half-mile south of a bridge crossing the Hoh River.) In 6 miles, turn left onto State Road H1000. Follow this road 10.5 miles to the trailhead, passing the South Fork Hoh Campground at 7.8 miles.

The great gulps of moisture that roll eastward from the Pacific to the shoulders of Mount Olympus, dropping an incredible 140 inches of precipitation a year along the South Fork of the Hoh River, have given rise to a startling world of green giants. This is without question the greatest untrammeled rain forest anywhere in the continental United States, and certainly the most accessible. There are portions of this walk that will leave you feeling like you're passing through one big ooze of chloroplast. It is Longfellow's "forest primeval," William Henry Hudson's "green mansions," and George Meredith's "enchanted woods" all rolled up into one. Of all the forest walks you will ever take, there is no forgetting the Hoh.

Our walk begins in a wash of sword and deer fern, salmonberry, oxalis, and trailing yellow violets—all growing at the feet of conifers and broadleaf maples dripping with thick curtains of club moss. The first conifer to greet you will be the Sitka spruce. Growing from the Alaskan Coast Ranges southward to the coast of California's Mendocino County, the Sitka attains tremendous stature here on the west side of the Olympic Peninsula; indeed, the second largest Sitka spruce in the world is found along the Lower Hoh River. It's not unusual to run across Sitkas 200 feet high and 10 feet in diameter, some of which have been growing for 800 years. One can hardly help but feel a little giddy at rubbing elbows with trees that were up and at it when Marco Polo was setting sail for China.

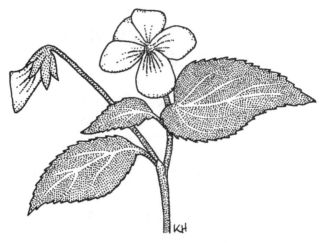

Yellow Violet

Sitka Spruce

As you settle into this walk, keep your ears and eyes open for a host of beautiful birds, including hairy woodpeckers, dark-eyed juncos, rufous hummingbirds, and winter wrens. If you do spot winter wrens here, it will probably be as they flit through shrubs and dense undergrowth searching for insects. More likely, though, is that you'll hear their song—a high, musical trill lasting for several seconds, and then repeating. One of the more intriguing behaviors of the winter wren is that the male builds a large nestlike structure complete with an entrance portal, usually in full view. The birds then nest somewhere else. Some ornithologists suspect that this initial structure may actually be a ruse meant to throw off animals and other birds that would prey on either the eggs or young birds. This little songster, incidentally, is the only wren whose range extends outside of the Americas.

Continue past hemlocks, spruce, and an occasional broadleaf maple, as well as blue huckleberry, buttercup, foamflower, skunk cabbage, and vanilla leaf, the latter plant easily identified by its three wavy-edged leaves that look something like the wings of a butterfly. True to its common name, the dried leaves of the plant do have an odor somewhat reminiscent of vanilla. At 1.2 miles you'll pass a lovely stream, its cool, sweet cargo bound for the South Fork of the Hoh, but not before passing dozens of rocks covered with tiny gardens of moss and oxalis. Oxalis, the plant that looks like a shamrock, is also known as wood sorrel. It was the wood sorrel (though of another variety) that many people believe to have been the original Irish shamrock—the plant that Saint Patrick used to explain the concept of Christian trinity to the Celts. For several centuries soldiers fastened sprigs of wood sorrel to their helmets or swords for protection against witches and other magicians—a practice that, at least when standing in this fantastic Druidscape of a rain forest, doesn't seem silly at all.

At 1.5 miles, roughly a mile after entering Olympic National Park, you'll come to Big Flat—a fine open area studded with several beautiful broadleaf maples. This park is kept clear for the most part by the ferocious appetites of Roosevelt elk, which waste no time nipping any young trees that try to get their start here. Olympic National Park contains one of the best herds of Roosevelt elk in America, consisting of several thousand animals. For a time, there was a strong push to name this preserve not Olympic, but Elk National Park. You'll have the best chance of seeing these regal animals if you're here in winter, since during the warm months they migrate up into the higher reaches of the Olympic Mountains.

Just before you leave this first park area, on your left will be a good example of what biologists refer to as a tree "colonade." Colonades are formed when several trees begin growing on top of a single fallen "nurse log." Eventually the nurse log rots away, and what is left is a long line of trees, the entire row looking very much as if it were planted. Sixty yards or so past this first open area is another opening, this one flanked on the left by a lovely stand of red alders. Red alders are often confused with birch trees, since they have a mottled white trunk like the birch, covered with crusty plates of lichen. (The only red coloring these trees can claim is their inner bark.) Red alder is like aspen in that it does extremely well reclaiming burned, insect-killed, or logged-over areas. Alas, its days are numbered; if no further disturbance of the area occurs, spruce, hemlock, and cedar will overtake it.

From this grove continue for about 150 yards, past an alder park framing the right side of the trail. At a point where the path comes fairly close to the South Fork of the Hoh River (a massive Douglas fir snag will be visible directly ahead of you), leave it and make your way to the bank of the river. This is a lovely, serene spot—a wonderful place to watch the summer light playing off the ripples of the river. Keep your eyes open for belted kingfishers, who do quite nicely dining on the smaller fish that live in this cool, clear waterway.

WALK #13—LEADBETTER POINT

DISTANCE: 1 mile
ENVIRONMENT: Coast
LOCATION: Willapa National Wildlife Refuge. From the town of Seaview, head north (at this point the road actually goes east) on U.S. Highway 101. In 0.5 mile, turn left (north) onto Sandridge Road. Follow this for 15.5 miles, to a "T" intersection at Stackpole Road. Turn left (west) onto Stackpole Road for 0.4 mile, past the Oysterville Store, and then turn right, following the signs for Leadbetter Point. Park in the lot farthest to the north, and pick up the trail that heads due north.

There's no doubt about it. Leadbetter Point, which comprises a unique mix of state park and Willapa National Wildlife Refuge lands, is a bird-lover's paradise. Though winter is among the best times to visit Leadbetter, much is happening here during other seasons as well. During peak periods of migration in the spring and fall, for instance, there are literally tens of thousands of birds—brants, sanderlings, turnstones—feeding and resting on the mud flats, marshes, and beaches of the point. In late summer you can see sooty shearwaters winging past on their incredible journey from the Aleutian Islands to nesting grounds off the coast of New Zealand. Since Mom and Dad Shearwater depart before their chicks have fledged, the young birds end up making the long trip back to the Aleutians on their own.

Don't pass up Leadbetter Point just because you may not be big on bird watching. Those who don't know an eagle from a sea goose still find the walking wonderful—easy, carefree strolling through a place thick with the joys of wild places. One note of caution, though. Hiking here in the summer means sharing the place with mosquitoes. If your visit occurs between May and September, wear lots of clothes, eat lots of garlic, and bring a generous supply of bug repellent.

A short distance from the parking area is an information sign, marking the beginning of a loop trail. We're not going to take this loop walk through the park, but will instead turn right here, toward the bay side of the peninsula. The short path from this sign down to the beach passes through leathery green mats of kinnikinnick. Kinnikinnick leaves were dried and smoked by Indians (and later settlers) throughout North America. The curious name comes from an Algonquian word meaning "smoking mixture," and refers to the fact that the leaves of kinnikinnick were typically mixed with several other kinds of plants, including red-osier dogwood,

Beach Pea

willow, and even tobacco. Folk healers have long prescribed kinnikinnick for treating infections of the bladder—a use warranted by the plant's high concentrations of an astringent known as arbutin.

Also along this path to the beach will be groves of shore pine (also known as lodgepole pine), as well as tufts of beach grass. Even though both of these plants are very good at stabilizing dune areas, the forces of wind and water bring a great many changes to the face of Leadbetter Point from year to year. Once you reach the beach and head north, watch the sandy ridges and depressions to your left for other plant life, including lupine, wild strawberry, beach pea, sea rocket, and gorse.

Note the lush islands of marsh plants growing in the salt flats to your right. One of these is a kind of pickleweed, and another is commonly referred to as arrowgrass. Despite the high level of nutrients found here, setting up shop in salty soil (the salinity here is roughly 5 percent), is not an option open to many. Those plants that manage it are called *halophytes*, and they survive the desiccating effects of salt only by employing some rather specialized equipment. For example, the leaves of halophytes are often covered with hairs, or even a waxy powder, that allows a higher intake and retention of fresh water. Some have leaf glands that actually remove the salt and deposit it on the outside, while others grow in shapes that reduce the amount of surface area exposed to the sun.

As each year passes, plants like pickleweed and arrowgrass are losing ground to an invader from the East Coast, known as smooth cordgrass. A robust, tenacious colonizer, smooth cordgrass is actually changing the face of the Leadbetter flats. By trapping sediments, it creates ground surfaces that are far less favorable to the food requirements of many migratory birds. A variety of measures to control the plant are now being tested.

These nutrient-rich mud flats are also prime habitat for many other kinds of life, including oysters, clams, and crabs. If you're here early in the morning, look for fresh raccoon tracks in the mud.

There is no specific turnaround point for this walk. Simply make your way out along the bay side of the refuge as far as you'd like, trying to keep track of all the different kinds of birds you see along the way. Do keep in mind that the northern fringe of Leadbetter Point along the ocean beachside is closed to all traffic from April through August. This is to protect nesting snowy plovers, which, as of late, are having increasing difficulty reproducing. Closing the area keeps people from inadvertently stepping on the snowy plover's eggs (they blend in extremely well with the sand), or frightening the plovers off their nests, which, of course, then leaves the eggs exposed to predators.

South–Central Washington

WALK #14—COLUMBIA GORGE OVERLOOK

DISTANCE: 1 mile
ENVIRONMENT: Mountain
LOCATION: Columbia Gorge National Scenic Area. From the intersection of state highways 14 and 141 in Bingen, drive east on Highway 14 for 4.4 miles. Turn left onto County Road 1230 (on the edge of Rowland Lake), and follow this for 1.6 miles to our trailhead, on the left side of the highway.

There are few places where one needs a bigger repertoire of superlatives to describe the landscape than the Columbia Gorge. Packed into this 80-mile-long canyon are five major vegetative zones, giving rise to a higher level of plant diversity than any other area in the Pacific Northwest. Here you'll find well over 700 flowering plants. Indeed, every twist of trail seems a doorway into a different world, one where light and shadow and precipitation mingle to create striking new combinations of life.

From the gate at the trailhead you'll see two faint roads: one takes off to the north (perpendicular to the highway), and the other runs generally east-northeast. For this walk we'll follow the northern route (the other path is described on page 51). We'll begin by traversing a gentle slope of wind-tossed grasses, which in spring are spiked with the lovely cream and lavender blooms of bicolored cluster lilies. In just 0.2 mile you'll pass through a line of trees; on your left look for ponderosa pine and black hawthorn, and on the right, white oak and Oregon ash. Curiously, in writings of the Northwest fur trade we find claims relating to how one never finds snakes—especially poisonous ones—near Oregon ash; in fact, this tree was said to so repel serpents that one had only to walk the fields and forests with an Oregon ash branch in hand to send them slithering for their lives. In all likelihood such beliefs were carryovers from earlier times; even Roman scholars suggested planting ash trees to discourage snakes.

Just past this line of trees turn left, continuing west on a faint roadbed. After roughly 50 yards this road disappears, at which point you should continue a westerly course, generally following a small lip of basalt that runs in a wavy line across the meadows. Just after the roadbed ends you'll cross a small hummock, which in spring is dotted with the exquisite blooms of bitterroot. The roots of this plant were long a favorite food of native peoples, especially in what is now western Montana and northern Idaho. Because roots are both more tender and more nutritious before the flowers appear, Indians would begin digging them with pointed sticks soon after the snow was melted. Typically, the first day of digging was ceremonial; a respected elder woman orchestrated the activity, and whatever plants were harvested were used in a feast of thanksgiving. Over the course of the season a family might unearth 50 to 70 pounds of bitterroot, much of which they dried for later use. Just to the north of this small hummock you may also find patches of camas lilies, flying deep-blue flowers from their stems. Camas was another extremely important food source—not just for natives, but for trappers and early settlers throughout the Northwest.

From this point our walk winds past small-flowered prairie stars to a seep rich with monkeyflowers; just to the north are clusters of lupine, which in early summer add splashes of blue to the greens and grays of the oak forest. In another 0.1 mile is a small north-south ridge. Climb over this ridge and continue walking west to our turnaround point—a rocky knoll of basalt, spiked with pussytoes and the beautiful Barrett's penstemon. PLEASE NOTE: Visitors with children should be aware that the south side of this lookout is flanked by sheer cliffs; use extreme caution.

From this viewpoint you can see the Gorge in all its glory. There are hills strewn with wildflowers, and across the river, long runs of apple orchards. To the south rich blankets of coniferous forests climb up into the mountains, while to the east are the sheer walls that mark the end of the Long Narrows. In the drainage immediately west of where you're standing are long ribbons of volcanic basalt. This entire region is a geological wonderland, a place scarred and textured by fiery volcanic eruptions, landslides, and even major floods. The Bretz Flood, which roared through here roughly 12,000 to 15,000 years ago, is thought to have been the largest in world history. An ice dam on Lake Missoula, located far to the east, suddenly gave way, sending nearly 400 cubic miles of water through this area in about 40 hours; incredibly, in this area the Columbia River was running about a thousand feet higher than the level you see it at today.

WALK #15—CATHERINE CREEK

DISTANCE: 1 mile
ENVIRONMENT: Forest
LOCATION: Columbia Gorge National Scenic Area. From the intersection of state highways 14 and 141 in Bingen, drive east on Highway 14 for 4.4 miles. Turn left onto County Road 1230 (on the edge of Rowland Lake), and follow this for 1.6 miles to our trailhead, on the left side of the highway. From the trailhead you'll see two faint roadbeds—one taking off to the north, perpendicular to the highway, and another running more east-northeast; Catherine Creek is reached via this latter route.

Whereas the Columbia Gorge Overlook Walk (page 49) offers a dose of the magnificent, nearby Catherine Creek shows an entirely different face: the peace and quiet of a stream cradled by oak, bigleaf maple, and ponderosa, flanked to the east by an abrupt wall of volcanic basalt. Here the feeling is one of back trails and shaded canyons, of untrammeled niches wrapped in the sounds of meadowlark, western bluebird, and Lewis' woodpecker.

The road you'll be walking is in fact an old wagon route, used for years by early settlers as a means of skirting the rock protrusions that pinched off westward travel along the north side of the river. Speaking of settlers, it's worth noting that you're standing very near the official terminus of the Oregon Trail, located across the river between The Dalles and Rowena. By the time emigrants reached this point they had been on the trail for roughly 2,000 miles—miles that often brought hunger, extraordinary physical hardship, and, on more than a few occasions, sickness and death. Though the westward movement began as a trickle, in the 20 years between 1840 and 1860 more than 50,000 people landed here via the Oregon Trail. (Thousands of others came west via ship, on a six-month journey around the cape of South America.)

The reasons people had for embarking on such a journey were, of course, varied. A financial panic in 1837 pushed a great many midwestern farmers into serious debt; indeed, poor farmers from the Mississippi River region made up a great portion of those who migrated to Oregon throughout the 1840s. What's more, several seasons of terrible flooding occurred in that area from 1836 to 1849, giving rise to severe outbreaks of malaria. The West, well steeped in lore about its "healthful climate," became increasingly attractive. (Not that the trail was free from disease. A cholera outbreak in St. Louis in 1849 spread rapidly westward, leaving a long line of graves along the route.)

Turning the dream of Oregon into reality was hardly a simple process. A good covered wagon made of hardwood and a team of eight oxen would set you back about $400; if you opted for six mules instead, the bill ran about $400 higher. (One of the many myths perpetuated by Hollywood is that Oregon-bound emigrants pulled their wagons with horses. Oxen were not only cheaper, but they didn't stampede easily and could cover distances far better than any horse.) Of course, once you had your team and wagon, you still had to outfit yourself and your family with $200 to $300 worth of supplies. There were food staples to buy, including flour, sugar, coffee, dried fruit, bacon, rice, and lard, and also equipment, such as a tent, cooking utensils, tools, candles, and soap.

Pack all this into a 4-by-10-foot wagon box, squeeze in whatever farm implements you could manage, and you can see that there was hardly enough room for the deluxe furnishings and late-night confabs featured in episodes of "Wagon Train." In most cases space was so tight that unless you were very sick or very young, you ended up traversing a lot of the Oregon Trail by foot.

The typical wagon train left the Missouri River Valley in April, timing the journey to catch good grass on the Great Plains, as well as to reach the Willamette Valley before winter. While it's true that many settlers worried about attacks from Indians, this proved to be far less of a danger than you might think; over the entire history of the Oregon Trail only 400 people died from encounters with Indians.

Unfortunately, there was one more hurdle between this spot and the Willamette Valley. Early emigrants had to either load everything onto rafts and attempt a dangerous float down the Columbia or get in line for a ride on one of the more seaworthy, passenger-carrying boats that plied the river. The latter choice meant that someone from the party had to stay behind and herd the animals, alternately wading through the edges of strong river currents and negotiating the narrow, slippery trails that clung to the walls of the gorge. In time, a man named Samuel Barlow built a road up and across the forested flanks of Mount Hood, but it generally lacked good feed and was in places thick with mud. One can only imagine the kind of euphoria that must have erupted as families finally reached the Willamette Valley.

It's worth noting that the primary reason this area was available for such massive settlement was because most of the native peoples had been killed off by introduced disease. In the western portions of the gorge alone, more than 90 percent of the native residents had died by the early 1800s, most from illnesses such as smallpox and measles. Before that time there was a thriving, vibrant blend of native cultures. Particularly fascinating was a stretch of river known as the Long Narrows, near The Dalles—a primary trading center of the Northwest. Though there were seldom more than a hundred full-time residents along this stretch, during fishing and trading season that number swelled to more than 3,000. People of the Puget Sound brought dentalia shells, baskets, canoes, and dried clams, while tribes from southern Oregon came with obsidian, Indian tobacco, and water lily seeds. Pipestone arrived from Minnesota, copper from Alaska or the Great Lakes, and turquoise from the Southwest.

Soon after you leave the trailhead, the road drops gently to the banks of Catherine Creek. In addition to the varied vegetation along the stream itself, on the hills to your left are nice patches of wildflowers. At 0.3 mile is a fork; stay right and cross Catherine Creek, taking a moment or two to enjoy these gentle plunge pools and moss-covered rocks. Once you cross the creek, on your right will be a sheer wall of basalt, softened at the base by a line of broadleaf maple. From here it's a short trek to our turnaround point at a weathered corral. Though quiet today, this corral once bustled with the activities of the Lauterbach Cattle Ranch.

Just east of this corral is a magnificent rock arch, located along a cleft line in the Yakima basalt that either eroded or somehow pulled away from the rest of the formation. Curiously, the Bretz Flood that roared through here 12,000 to 15,000 years ago, when an ice dam gave way at mammoth Lake Missoula, may have also played some kind of role in shaping this arch. Proof of the flood can be found about halfway up the north cleft of the arch, where there remains a large granite boulder, deposited here by the raging waters.

WALK #16—LEWIS RIVER

DISTANCE: 5.6 miles
ENVIRONMENT: Forest
LOCATION: Gifford Pinchot National Forest. From Interstate 5 north of Vancouver, take exit 21 and head east on State Highway 503. Near the town of Cougar, go east on Forest Road 90 for about 40 miles to Lower Falls Campground. Our walk takes off from the northeast corner of the camping area.

If ever you find yourself overwhelmed by how rapidly the natural areas of the Northwest are being lost to development, if your own good fight for wild places seems to be turning heavy and sour, then come to Lewis River. This is a healing place. It is Washington at its very best—a splendid, unfettered watercourse, dancing like a prima ballerina through hushed woodlands pleated with ferns and flowers. And if, like Izaak Walton, you're a person who loves "any discourse with rivers," then I can promise that your walk along the Lewis will be one of the finest conversations you'll ever have.

Starting from the cold bellies of glaciers lying on the western side of Mount Adams, the Lewis traverses a number of beautiful places, bringing flushes of life to its banks all the way to the western edge of the Gifford Pinchot National Forest. A mere 50 years ago, the "natural" feeling of the area extended well past even that. For instance, the 1941 *WPA Guide to Washington* boasts that around Merwin Reservoir "first-growth timber still crowns the hillsides;" that the surrounding area "abounds with duck, pheasant, bear and deer;" and that farther west toward Woodland, "strawberries, raspberries, youngberries, and cranberries grow in generous quantities." (Youngberries, in case you're wondering, were a cross between a trailing blackberry and a southern dewberry.) "The fields yield heavy crops of peas, garden vegetables, and alfalfa. Dairy farms and poultry ranches, where many turkey are raised, also thrive on the countryside."

From the trailhead parking area at Lower Falls Campground, head upstream on trail 31, which is cradled by vanilla leaf, three-leafed anemone, pipsissewa, bunchberry, and the small greenish flowers of broad-leaved twayblades. The flower of this latter plant has a small, coiled mechanism with a sticky ball of pollen attached. A visiting insect triggers the coil, which then shoots the pollen onto its body; the pollen is then carried to other twayblade flowers for fertilization. There are actually three kinds of twayblades in western North America, and Washington has them all. A good clue to recognizing any twayblade is the pair of opposite leaves growing about halfway up the stem.

Soon the path climbs onto a bench sitting high above the river. While there are times when the water is lost from sight, it's never lost from sound; the hiss and rumble of one set of rapids never quite fades out before another takes its place. One of the reasons for this is the formation of the riverbed, which in places consists of flat slabs of volcanic rock stacked on top of each other like fallen dominos. By 0.4 mile you can look down from your elevated position into a shaded floodplain thick with carpets of sword fern. Overhead lie scattered groves of Pacific silver fir and Douglas fir, as well as an occasional alder, hemlock, and western redcedar.

The rather sorry-looking bridge visible on the right about 0.2 mile after this lowland garden is known as Old Sheep Bridge, and it was used primarily by sheep ranchers and miners to access the east side of the Lewis River. In 1968 a mud slide roared down the valley north of here, damming the Lewis River. When the dam finally broke, the Lewis came through like a rocket, taking the bridge ramps with it. Since mining and grazing activity had pretty well subsided by then, the bridge was never rebuilt; the Forest Service is, however, considering constructing a pedestrian crossing here.

If by now the whole place has started to massage you into a fine state of lethargy, just past the old bridge is a delightful stopping point. Here, a lovely little stream comes laughing out of an alder-covered hillside, finally plunging with a fine hiss over a 15-foot precipice. Bedstraw and yellow monkeyflower are plentiful here, as is Siberian miner's lettuce—a plant bearing blooms of five notched white petals with red lines.

Also growing here are some few nice broadleaf maples. The large, deeply lobed leaves of this tree have shaded many a western Washington neighborhood against the sizzle of summer. In spring,

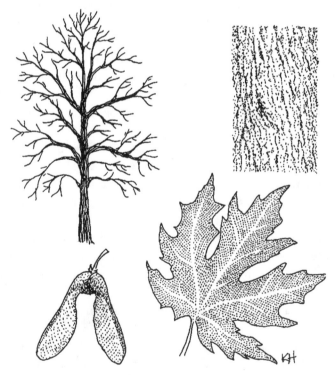

Broadleaf Maple

about the time that the leaves are 80 percent grown, the broadleaf maple sends out delicate clusters of drooping, bright yellow flowers. Though these flowers soon fade, color returns to the tree again in the fall, when its leaves glow with yellow and orange. During the heyday of fur trapping in the Northwest, the men of the Hudson's Bay Company were especially fond of gun stocks carved from this tree.

After yet another warm-up waterfall on Copper Creek at 1.5 miles, you'll come to Middle Falls—a splendid, Niagaralike cascade split by a smooth tongue of rock. Those who have little time or energy can turn around here, though I promise you that the additional mile to the Upper Falls is worth every step. The trail climbs sharply beyond Middle Falls but then levels out again, offering much the same kind of walk that you've had thus far. Added to the scene, though, is an abundance of springs flowing out of the trailside rocks, in one case creating a high, vertical wall draped with an exquisite array of tiny ferns and brilliant green tufts of moss—each with clear, cool water dripping off the tips.

As for the Upper Falls of the Lewis, they are indescribably beautiful. The river literally thunders over high cliffs into a large emerald plunge pool, the whole scene framed by mammoth trunks of redcedar. This is wild water, crashing out of a grand, green forest with total abandon. I dare say that were you to see this scene in a painting, it would probably appear the work of wishful thinking. For all the walking you have ever done or are yet to do, this place, this dazzling slice of wild, will lay long and lovely in your memories of the Northwest.

> What would the world be, once bereft
> Of wet and wildness? Let them be left ...
> —*Gerard Manley Hopkins*

WALK #17—HARMONY VIEWPOINT

DISTANCE: 2.4 miles
ENVIRONMENT: Mountain
LOCATION: Mount Saint Helens National Volcanic Monument, in the Gifford Pinchot National Forest. From the town of Randle on U.S. Highway 12, head south on State Highway 131 for 2 miles; continue south on Forest Road 25 for 18 miles to Forest Road 99, and turn right (west). Follow this for 13.6 miles to Harmony Viewpoint, located on the right side of the road. Our walk is along the Harmony Falls Trail.

The staggering effects of the Mount Saint Helens blast are readily apparent to anyone driving Forest Road 99 through the monument. But to walk off the lip of Harmony Viewpoint, or to stand on the shore of Spirit Lake and stare into the collapsed face of Mount Saint Helens, is to feel completely immersed in the place. Even on bright days the volcano seems tired and haggard, her once shimmering flanks thick with a gray drizzle of ash. It remains to be seen whether she's too tired to blow her stack again, sending her recently constructed, 1,000-foot-high lava dome spewing into the Washington sky.

As stark as the images along this walk can be, it's hard not to be amazed at the amount of life springing from the slopes beneath the highway. To some extent, this face was spared the full impact of the blast because of the protection offered by the high ridge on your left. Also in its favor is the fact that it faces generally northward—an orientation that allows it to retain more rain and snowfall than its south-facing counterpart on the other side of the valley.

Beside patches of fireweed, huckleberry, and dwarf bramble you'll find alder, western mountain ash, trailing blackberry, and elderberry. In spring and early summer the wildflowers are delightful—lone splashes of color in a muted landscape. Look for the large, single white flowers of trillium and queen's cup, as well as the ivory-colored blooms of vanilla leaf, devil's club, false Solomon's seal, and western mountain ash. At a crook in the trail at 0.6 mile, near a place where a small spray of water trickles down an outcrop

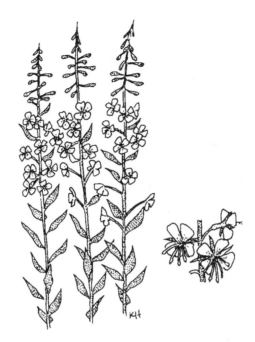

Fireweed

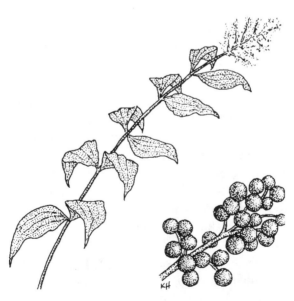

False Solomon's Seal

Bunchberry

of rock, the garden gets even brighter. Here you'll find the rose-colored blooms of bleeding heart, the pleated petals of Oregon fairy bells, and a little farther down the trail, a fine weave of bunchberry. This latter plant is a member of the dogwood family; in August it sports clusters of bright red berries, a favorite of white-tailed deer.

By 1.1 miles the path will have largely faded into a gray, barren mound of ash, leaving you to follow a series of posts to the shore of a small inlet stream. This little watercourse, its banks lined with lavender tufts of lupine and the scarlet of red monkeyflower, seems completely nonplussed by the surrounding devastation. It gurgles strongly and clearly into Spirit Lake, offering its waters to various grasses and willows, all of which are slowly reclaiming the land.

On May 17, 1980, Spirit Lake was still a clear, cold mountain lake—high on oxygen and low on nutrients. But the blast the next day changed all that. For starters, part of the volcano's north side actually fell into the lake, raising the water level by almost 200 feet. Secondly, both the explosion and the resulting debris caused waves to form that crashed against nearby ridges to heights more than 800 feet above the original lake level! The actual surface area of the lake almost doubled, from 1,300 acres to 2,500 acres.

Carbon, iron, sulfur, ammonium, and manganese were carried into the lake by rainfall and snowmelt, causing an explosion of bacterial activity that greatly depleted oxygen levels. (This process was speeded up by drastic increases in the water temperature; the day after the blast, Spirit Lake had a temperature of 91 degrees— a full 40 degrees higher than it would have normally been at that time of year.) Gradually, these new nutrients were depleted and temperatures dropped. Oxygen was stirred back into the water both by wind and by the mixing that occurs in lakes due to seasonal temperature changes.

Because Spirit Lake was so close to the inner blast zone, fish and amphibian life were destroyed. However, at the time, various kinds of frogs and toads were hibernating in the bottoms of other, more protected lakes and streams. Their progeny quickly found their way into Spirit Lake, and have been successfully reproducing there ever since. Also, a great many ant colonies survived beneath the ground, while beetles and ballooning spiders (spiders that travel on the winds using silken "parachutes") arrived in great numbers. It wasn't long before Roosevelt elk and black-tailed deer were also seen here, having migrated in from surrounding lands to feed on the surviving vegetation.

Though it can seem like a slow process to those of us who measure time by hours and weeks and months, there has in fact been a tremendous resurgence of life at Mount Saint Helens. In fact, one of the biggest surprises to scientists was how many species survived what at first seemed total devastation. In turn, the survival of these species in the years that followed has been aided by the large amounts of organic material wrapped in this shattered landscape.

WALK #18—INDEPENDENCE PASS

DISTANCE: 0.5 mile
ENVIRONMENT: Mountain
LOCATION: Mount Saint Helens National Volcanic Monument, in the Gifford Pinchot National Forest. From the town of Randle on U.S. Highway 12, head south on State Highway 131 for 2 miles; continue south on Forest Road 25 for 18 miles to Forest Road 99, and turn right (west). Follow this for 12.2 miles to Independence Pass Interpretive Trail, located on the right side of the road.

It wasn't as if the eruption of Mount Saint Helens on that fine Sunday morning in May 1980 was a complete surprise. Two months earlier, there had been a series of shallow earthquakes on the north side of the mountain, followed by releases of steam that ripped a crater through the volcano's ice cap. As time went on, more and more earthquakes rumbled—thousands of them, in fact—and a crater formed at the summit, growing rapidly to 1,000 feet across. There was a large bulge on the volcano's north flank, which on some days swelled by more than 8 feet—a certain sign that viscous magma was rising high into the cone. Officials became concerned. First they closed the mountain to visitors, followed by an ever-widening circle of land around it.

And yet, when at 8:32 on May 18 an earthquake began to rumble on the mountain, no one—scientist, visitor, or nearby resident—could have imagined what was to follow. Twenty seconds later the entire north side of the volcano gave way, steamrolling down the mountain at 150 miles per hour, filling in, in less than 10 minutes, a 20-square-mile slice of the North Fork Toutle River Valley to an average depth of 150 feet. It was the largest landslide in recorded history. Later, flows of gas, ash, and pumice—some of it 1,100 degrees Fahrenheit—poured out of the volcano, killing virtually every bit of life and organic material on the northern fringe of the mountain. Even 15 miles distant the blast thundered along at speeds from 200 to over 600 miles per hour, snapping 3-foot-thick Douglas firs like they were so many matchsticks; by the time it was all over, enough timber had been blown down to build 300,000 two-bedroom houses.

By the time the main Mount Saint Helens eruptions were over, the amount of fallen ash would have buried a football field 150 miles deep. Some of it was thrown high into the atmosphere, circling the earth in 15 days. Two hundred homes were damaged or destroyed, as were 27 bridges and 185 miles of road. More than 30 ships were stranded in the Columbia, volcanic debris having choked the river into a channel one-third as deep and wide as it had been before the blast. Fifty-seven people were dead or missing. After 123 years of silence, Mount Saint Helens had spoken with a roar heard around the world.

Since the time of the original blast, an easily visible lava dome has built up within the crater, measuring more than 1,000 feet high and 3,000 feet wide. Such features are formed in two ways: first, magma rises into the core of the dome, making it swell; second, the hard crust of the dome breaks, allowing the molten rock to pour out and form rounded piles of lava. At the current rate of growth, this lava dome may grow enough to fill the excavated crater in a couple hundred years.

This short walk climbs for 0.2 mile to the top of a ridge affording splendid views of both Mount Saint Helens and Spirit Lake, much of it choked with downed timber. Though the regrowth of plants isn't as far along here as in other parts of the monument, you'll see fireweed, dwarf bramble, huckleberry, and some valiant little Pacific silver firs. These plants represent the beginning of a roughly 200-year-long process of reestablishing the old forests that existed in the undisturbed areas of the monument before the eruption. Though no human-aided reforestation is being done within the monument, on nearby national forest lands more than 10 million trees have been planted on abut 14,000 acres.

Continue along the ridge for another 50 yards to an interpretive area framed by benches. The information sign here is especially helpful to first-time visitors, outlining the location of several natural features, as well as where certain structures stood before the blast. No matter how many feet of videotape you saw flash across your television screen, no matter how many pictures you stared at in magazines and newspapers, there is simply no way to comprehend the awesome effect of the Mount Saint Helens eruption until you stand here and see it for yourself. In this one scene, consisting of miles and miles of toppled trees and ash-laden valleys peppered with flushes of green, is the whole story of Mount Saint Helens—a cycle of destruction, countered by the slow, patient push of new life.

WALK #19—SILVER FALLS

DISTANCE: 1.4 miles
ENVIRONMENT: Forest
LOCATION: Mount Rainier National Park. From Enumclaw (east of Tacoma), follow State Highway 410 for about 42 miles, to its junction with State Highway 123, on the east side of the park. From this junction, follow Highway 123 south for about 11 miles to the Stevens Canyon Entrance Road. Turn right (west) here, and go past the national park entrance station about 0.1 mile to a parking area on the right. Our walk takes off across the road and about 50 yards to the west.

If Minnehaha's father had used Silver Falls as the inspiration for naming his daughter in Longfellow's "The Song of Hiawatha," you can bet she wouldn't have come out with a name that means "laughing water." Thundering water, perhaps—crazy, hysterical water, maybe. But not laughing. (Curiously, Laughingwater Creek enters the river a short distance below Silver Falls.) I first visited here in the third week of June, and I must confess that I've rarely seen a cascade so splendidly out of control, frothing at its banks with complete and utter abandon. At the far edge of the plunge pool was a large collection of Douglas fir and cedar logs. Each had been pounded and pummeled by the Ohanapecosh River until it was free of every scrap of bark and branches—not unlike rocks tossed in a gem tumbler.

These late spring and early summer torrents of water serve as firm reminders that Mount Rainier is a place with no shortage of

Olive-sided Flycatcher

moisture. The highest seasonal snowfall in the world was recorded west of here, at Paradise, during the winter of 1971 and 1972—a staggering 93.5 feet. (The average annual snowfall is about half that, which still makes it a very snowy place.) With that amount of white stuff in the high country, you can't help but have significant runoff in the spring; in years when the warm weather comes in fast, some of these streams run down the mountain like runaway freight trains.

This path is more open than the one leading to Grove of the Patriarchs (see page 67), allowing shrubs such as huckleberry to flourish. Also here are wood and deer ferns, pipsissewa, Oregon grape, bunchberry, and devil's club, the latter plant brandishing spines on its stems and formidable thorns on the tops and bottoms of its large leaves.

Turn up your ears during the initial, relatively quiet portions of this trek for the sound of birds. The various canopy layers in a mixed conifer forest are really life zones—distinct vertical bands providing food and shelter for different kinds of birds, each of which has specific eating and nesting habits. In the low shrub layer of the forest will be found song sparrows, rufous-sided towhees, brown creepers, and Wilson's warblers, all of which glean both food and shelter close to the ground. Up high, on the other hand, feeding on insects found in and around the tree canopy, are birds like the olive-sided flycatcher and western tanager. (Note that it's primarily birds that live in the protection of high canopies that wear vivid colors, like the western tanager; birds nesting close to the ground are plainer looking, having a greater need to blend in with their surroundings.)

By 0.5 mile you'll see a small side trail taking off to the left, which will give you a view of the riotous cascades that brew and boil just before the plunge of Silver Falls. Returning to the main trail, continue along the river for another 0.2 mile, where you'll see a pathway taking off to your left, leading to a marvelous view of Silver Falls. Along the way look for salal, evergreen huckleberry, western redcedar, and Oregon grape, as well as shiny tufts of beargrass. Because beargrass tends to bloom only every few years,

Beargrass

during some visits you may see nothing but low, shaggy mats of grass (tasty looking, but unpalatable to most big game). In other years, it seems that every plant is topped by a 3-foot-tall flower stalk, each one waving a beautiful cluster of white blooms.

PLEASE NOTE: The railings around the Silver Falls viewpoint are there for your safety. Several people have died in these waters trying to climb out on the wet rocks for a better view.

WALK #20—GROVE OF THE PATRIARCHS

DISTANCE: 1.5 miles
ENVIRONMENT: Forest
LOCATION: Mount Rainier National Park. From Enumclaw (east of Tacoma), follow State Highway 410 for about 42 miles, to a junction with State Highway 123, on the east side of the park. From this junction, follow Highway 123 south for about 11 miles to the Stevens Canyon Entrance Road. Turn right (west) here, and go past the national park entrance station about 0.1 mile to a large parking area on the right (north) side of the road. Our walk takes off from here, heading north.

It boggles the mind to think that when some of the trees you'll meet on this walk first poked their heads above the soil, Viking raider Leif Erickson was about to reach the North American continent. When King John's arm was being twisted into signing the Magna Carta, or Ferdinand and Isabella were presiding over the horrors of the Spanish Inquisition, some of these Douglas firs and western redcedars had already seen 200 years drift across the Ohanapecosh River Valley. And by the time that Captain George Vancouver "discovered" mighty Mount Rainier in the spring of 1792, these trees were splendid, herculean giants. Today this forest remains among the most magnificent old growth areas in the entire Northwest—a haunting destination that will steal the breath of even the most jaded outdoor traveler.

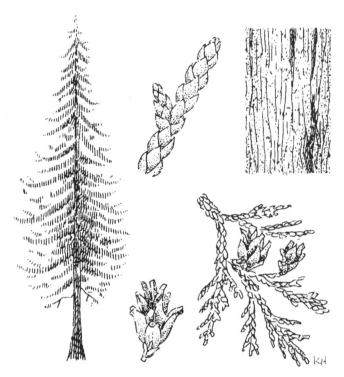

Western Redcedar

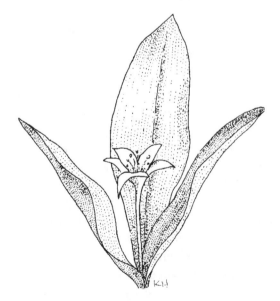

Queen's Cup

The two largest trees you'll see on this walk are Douglas fir and western redcedar, 30 of which measure more than 25 feet in circumference; one redcedar—a staggering 35 feet around—is among the largest trees in the entire park. (Redcedar is also sometimes called "canoe-cedar"—a reference to coastal Indians having used it for making canoes. Indeed, the art of canoe-building never reached a higher level than it did in the coastal tribes of Washington and British Columbia. Voyaging canoes were up to 65 feet long, bore three masts, and could carry between 30 and 40 people.) You'll also see plenty of hemlocks throughout this trek, though they reach nowhere near the same proportions as redcedar and Douglas fir.

On your way to the Grove of the Patriarchs you'll pass a variety of plants, most of which will show up on other walks nearby. Look for twisted stalk, bunchberry, salmonberry, devil's club, trillium, vanilla leaf, starflower, foamflower, and queen's cup. You'll recognize this latter plant by its two or three smooth green leaves, 6 to 8 inches long. Following the arrival in May or June of one white, six-petaled flower about an inch across, queen's cup produces a hard, oval-shaped berry in the most beautiful shade of blue.

Rounding out the common flora are tufts of strawberry leaves, graceful vine and broadleaf maples, and the large, soft leaves of thimbleberry, once used to a make a tea for treating anemia. There are also some wonderful clusters of ferns here, their soft fronds lending a delicate touch to a world ruled by giants. Ferns reproduce not by seeds but by tiny spores. Hundreds of thousands—in some species even millions—of these spores are produced each season. Spores are held in tiny cases, many of which are heaped together into tiny dots known as *sori*. It's these sori, or "fruit dots," that appear as dark-colored spots on the underside of fertile leaflets. It's usually dry when fern spore are released, allowing them to disperse over a wider range. Those that land in the right setting and at the right temperature will soon begin developing into a small plant called a *prothallus*. This prothallus has both male and female organs; once sperm is released and united with an egg, the egg then begins developing into what will become a new fern.

During the Renaissance, a belief known as the Doctrine of Signatures became a steering philosophy of medicine and general folklore for centuries to come. This doctrine basically said that plants bear certain signs, or "signatures," meant to instruct people as to their medical use. In the case of ferns, because the spores—the "seeds" of the plant—were so tiny, it was long believed that those who carried or ate them would also be made invisible.

Two of several ferns you'll be passing on this walk are wood fern and sword fern. Both were used by Northwest Indians to treat skin injuries; the roots of the wood fern were mashed and put on cuts, while spore cases were collected from the underside of sword fern fronds and placed on burns.

At 0.5 mile is a fork in the trail. Stay to the right, and cross a bridge over a fork of the Ohanapecosh River to a lovely grove of red alder. Soon you'll be in the thick of both standing and fallen old growth, the root systems of the latter rising into the air like some kind of wild modern art. At 0.6 mile is a small loop trail, where you'll bear to the right through the heart of the Grove of the Patriarchs.

If you find this particular cathedral too busy for your tastes, then return to the trail junction at 0.4 mile (this is the one you came to just before crossing the bridge over the Ohanapecosh River). The trail running north makes a nice meander along the west bank of the Ohanapecosh. While you won't find the trees along this path to be as large as they were on the island, they nonetheless form a magnificent and thoroughly enchanting forest.

WALK #21—CARBON GLACIER

DISTANCE: 6.8 miles
ENVIRONMENT: Mountain
LOCATION: Mount Rainier National Park, Wonderland Trail. From the town of Buckley, head south on State Road 165. In 10.5 miles you'll come to a fork; take the left branch, following signs toward the Carbon River entrance to Mount Rainier National Park and Ipsut Creek Campground. Our trail takes off from a parking area on the east side of Ipsut Creek Campground, which lies 13.2 miles from this last road junction.

Given the fact that Mount Rainier contains the largest mountain glacier system in the continental United States, it would be hard to imagine a more appropriate place to rub elbows with these great sculptors of the high country. At about 4 square miles in size, Carbon Glacier is the second largest in the park, as well as the most accessible. (Top honors for size go to Emmons Glacier, 5 square miles, and the biggest glacier in the country outside of Alaska.) Altogether, there are more than 30 square miles of ice covering various portions of this mighty mountain, dropping down from its upper reaches like the spokes of a wheel.

The creation of glaciers is related not so much to extreme cold as to those times when more snow falls in the winter than can melt in the summer. As the snow layers grow deeper and deeper, their weight eventually begins to compact them into hard glacial ice— ice, though, with a certain give to its bottom layers, which allows it to begin moving downslope. (Research in Glacier National Park found that, generally speaking, glaciers begin to move when they've grown to a thickness of at least 100 feet.) There was a time when the Rainier ice sheets were literally thousands of feet thick; bulldozing their way slowly downslope, they cut the beautiful, deep "U"-shaped valleys and the staggering vertical cliffs you see today, including magnificent Willis Wall, which lies at the head of Carbon Glacier. So while forces deep inside the earth may have created this mountain in the first place, it was glaciers that lent such dramatic beauty to its final form, slicing and polishing it like a sculptor pulling his or her tools across a lump of clay.

Our trail begins in a lovely forest of Douglas fir. Here the bottomlands are cut by an abundance of streams, each more fully framed by blooms, leaves, and fern fronds than the last. Deer fern, wood fern, and sword fern are common here, as are foamflower, bunchberry, queen's cup, star-flowered Solomon's seal, twisted stalk, and huckleberry. At about 0.2 mile, just past a small footbridge, is a trail junction; bear to the left toward Carbon Glacier, making a 0.1-mile climb up a small hill. At the top, the path traverses a bench overlooking a stream bottom. This is an ethereal place, where sunlight fingers plush carpets of fern, devil's club, and in summer, the silky green leaves and pink flower spikes of corydalis.

At 0.75 mile the trail reaches an opening at the edge of the Carbon River, with 5,000-foot-high Chenuis Mountain visible to the northeast. Watch trailside for vanilla leaf, hemlock, alder, and coltsfoot. A half-mile mile later you'll come across an avalanche path on the right side of the trail. Avalanche paths are intriguing places, since the absence of trees allows many plants to thrive here that wouldn't otherwise. This is a good spot to see salmonberry and alder, and beneath their branches, lovely splashes of foamflower, Siberian miner's lettuce, columbine, and maidenhair fern. The leaves of this latter plant were used by both Northwest Indians and European herbalists to treat congestion, coughs, and other irritations of the throat and chest.

By 2.5 miles you'll have gained wonderful views of Mount Rainier. The sky is pierced by peaks and ridgelines, and thin veils of water pour off the steep sides of Chenuis Mountain. One minute the air is chilled with the breath of Carbon River and Glacier, and the next it grows warm, almost sultry, laced with the smell of moisture-loving plants.

One plant you'll see along the right side of the trail here is vine maple, a modest tree that can be easily overlooked. In spring, though, vine maple sports clusters of red to purple flowers drooping from the ends of short twigs; in fall it becomes one of the loveliest of all the Northwest trees, splashing the forest with red and gold. Such beauty was all but lost on French fur trappers, who sometimes referred to vine maple as "devil of the forest," so called because its low-growing trunks tended to trip them as they made their way along portage trails. Indian tribes of this region used the branches of vine maple to make scoop nets for catching salmon.

At 3.2 miles you'll cross Cataract Creek, leaping and bounding out of Mist Park in a ribbon of froth. Two-tenths mile later is our turnaround point, at a cable bridge crossing the Carbon River. From here you can look upstream right into the snout of Carbon Glacier. The ice pack here isn't white, as you might have expected, but the shade of mud and ash, so colored by tons of sediment and till. If you want to get an even closer look, cross the bridge and go right, climbing rather sharply to a point beside the glacier's leading edge.

WALK #22—MOUNT LILLIAN TRAIL

DISTANCE: 2.2 miles
ENVIRONMENT: Mountain
LOCATION: Wenatchee National Forest. From U.S. Highway 2 west of the town of Wenatchee, turn south onto U.S. Highway 97. In approximately 22 miles, turn left (south) onto Forest Road 9716. Follow this for 3.8 miles, and turn left onto Forest Road 9712. In 5.7 miles you'll reach our trailhead (trail 1204), on the left side of the road. *Note:* A short distance to the east of this trailhead is a small road that actually parallels our trail. If you can't find a parking place on Forest Road 9712, you may want to pull onto the shoulder of this small road and walk back to our trailhead.

I should tell you from the start that the Mount Lillian Trail isn't fast-food walking—you know, the kind where you make a quick turn off the highway, grab a few yards of trail, and be back on the road again before the rubber on your tires has had a chance to cool. The 10 miles of twisting, sometimes confusing dirt roads that must be navigated to get to this path creates an experience more suitable to those who consider themselves eclectic, gourmet walkers—the kind of people who like to cruise back streets of strange towns for home cooking, instead of always heading for the Golden Arches.

Those who do have the time and patience to take this trail will be rewarded with a marvelous view into hundreds of square miles of dry, delicious landscape east of the Cascade Mountains—a complex symphony of rock and timber, sage and sky.

Like the scenery, the forest you'll be walking through on your way to the turnaround point is a rather hard-to-define mix. Engelmann spruce, subalpine fir, and lodgepole pine are all common, but in places, these are seasoned with sprinkles of whitebark pine and ponderosa. Underneath that are sparse, yet engaging gardens of yarrow, grouse whortleberry, pearly everlasting, and pyrola.

As you make your way along the first portion of this walk, you'll see lots of conifers draped with the dark, stringy hairs of

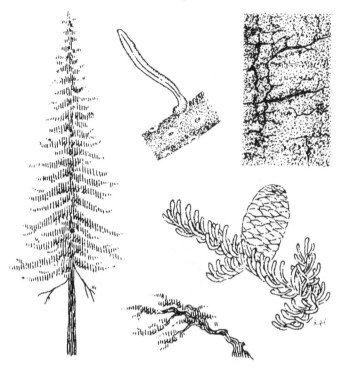

Subalpine Fir

black tree lichen. While few of us would ever describe this plant as appetizing, there was a time when the sweet taste of black tree lichen was enjoyed by many native families, especially during winter when other plants were scarce. After being cleaned, tree lichen was baked in a fire pit, which changed it into a smooth black mass. This could then be eaten as is, or else dried in the sun and ground into a sweet powder, to be used as an additive to other foods.

Two trees along this trail that serve as hat racks for black tree lichen are the subalpine fir and Engelmann spruce. Notice in the thick stands of timber how the lower reaches of the trees are bare of vegetation, lined only with the spikes of dead, gray limbs. This is a kind of self-pruning. It makes little sense to put effort into growing needles in a dark understory, when almost all the sunlight—and thus the energy—is to be had topside. In some forests, these rows of dead limbs will rise for more than a hundred feet, leaving just a tuft of food-producing vegetation waving high overhead.

At 0.4 mile you'll join the road that's been off to your right. A short distance later, take off to the right on trail 1601 and begin a moderate climb for 0.3 mile. There are some nice lodgepole pines in here, a few of the young ones sporting patches of sticky, tar-colored gunk on the tips of their lower branches. This is a mold that sometimes takes hold when the supple lower branches of a conifer are pinned to the ground for a prolonged period of time by heavy snow. Of course, as the tree grows, it will have fewer branches down low that can be caught in this compromising position. (One of the reasons that mountain conifers tend to have supple branches rising to a point, like a cone, is to shed snow.)

At 1.1 miles you'll come out of the forest into a small opening. On your left will be a faint trail leading in just 20 or 30 yards to a beautiful sandstone outcropping. Follow this to our turnaround point, on the edge of a high, windswept rim offering dazzling views of the country lying to the north, east, and west. At this point you'll be near the summit of Mount Lillian; if you're feeling adventurous, you can walk roughly 0.5 mile farther to the east, where you'll find a fascinating collage of sandstone formations, well worth exploring.

North–Central Washington

WALK #23—HIDDEN LAKE

DISTANCE: 1.1 miles

ENVIRONMENT: Forest

LOCATION: Wenatchee National Forest. From the town of Leavenworth, head west on U.S. Highway 2 for approximately 14 miles, and turn right (east) onto State Road 207. In about 4 miles, turn left (west) onto Forest Road 6607, which runs along the south side of Lake Wenatchee. Our trail takes off from the very end of Forest Road 6607, at Glacier View Campground.

The walk to Hidden Lake is one of those delightful forest treks that offer beauty from the very first step. Though for most of its 0.55-mile route this trail is an uphill affair, rest assured you'll never be but a step or two away from either engaging vegetation or a cool, deep view of Lake Wenatchee, shimmering through the spruce-fir forest. In the early morning or evening hours you can also count on a nice medley of birdsong, including some rather sweet-sounding numbers by mountain chickadees, red-breasted nuthatches, cedar waxwings, evening grosbeaks, rufous-sided to-whees, dark-eyed juncos, and downy woodpeckers; also on the program are more raucous offerings, courtesy of gray and Steller's jays, Clark's nutcrackers, and pileated and hairy woodpeckers. If you arrive at Hidden Lake at dusk, count on seeing some rather impressive acrobatics by swallows and brown bats.

The walk begins in a mix of grand fir, queen's cup, Oregon grape, twisted stalk, trillium, false Solomon's seal, pyrola, bracken fern, and devil's club. Devil's club, which is actually a relative of Asian ginseng, is appropriately named, as anyone knows who's had the misfortune of brushing up against the nasty barbs and spines that line its stems and leaf veins. (The Latin name of the plant—*Oplopanax horridum*—means "horrible weapon.") Nevertheless, this was an important plant to many of the native peoples of Washington, who used it for everything from treating diabetes to preventing head lice. What's more, deer and elk absolutely relish devil's club; in fact, if you want to see either of these animals, one of the best ways is to conceal yourself in the bottom of a valley or shaded ravine, where devil's club is most often found.

At 0.4 mile you'll run across a fine cluster of ponderosa. Though it's more common to see this tree in drier areas—areas receiving as little as 13 to 14 inches of moisture per year—it can actually tolerate twice that much precipitation. The only catch is that when ponderosa does set up shop in areas of higher moisture, it will only do so in sunny, well-drained soils.

One of the reasons this area is so special when it comes to plant life is that it happens to be sandwiched between two very different precipitation zones, and freely borrows residents from both. Lake Wenatchee typically gets about 40 inches of moisture a year, and Leavenworth, to the east, gets 24. Meanwhile, Steven's Pass, just to the west, may get 80!

Just about the time you've had enough climbing, the trail flattens out on the spine of a small ridge. Behind and well below you are the waters of Lake Wenatchee, while directly in front,

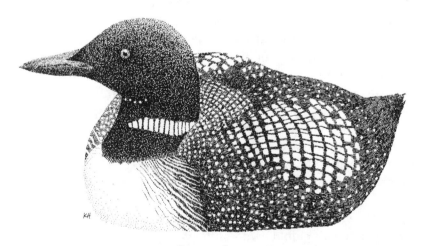

Common Loon

framing Hidden Lake, is a striking ponderosa park spiked with lupine, pipsissewa, and starflower. On the other side of the lake is a lacy mix of cedar and fir, the latter tree rising in dizzy leaps and bounds up the sheer cliffs that rise along the south side, crowning at 6,000-foot-high Nason Ridge.

If you're lucky, you may spot a loon in the quiet waters of Hidden Lake. Curiously, the bones of loons are more solid and weighty than those of other birds. In much the way that divers wear weight belts to better match themselves to the relative gravity of water, the loon's more massive bones allow it to make deep dives with ease. Of all the sounds that still float through the American outback, from the bugle of elk to the call of Canada geese, none can prickle the skin like the wild, haunting laugh of the loon.

WALK #24—BAGLEY LAKES

DISTANCE: 2.2 miles
ENVIRONMENT: Mountain
LOCATION: Chain Lakes Trail, in the Mount Baker–Snoqualmie National Forest. From the town of Bellingham, drive east for approximately 60 miles on State Highway 542 (Mount Baker Highway). Our walk takes off from a parking area located on the right side of the road, directly across from the main Mount Baker ski area building. Follow signs for the Chain Lakes Trail.

Admittedly, it was downright sporting of Captain George Vancouver to name magnificent Mount Baker after the third lieutenant in his expedition—the first man to spot the peak through a spyglass in April of 1792. The native peoples of this area, however, tended to be much more pragmatic in assigning names to things. Nooksack Indians, for instance, knew this mountain as *Koma-Kulshan*, which translates roughly into "white, shining, steep mountain." Indeed, Mount Baker towers 10,778 feet above the sea, supports a dozen glaciers and more than 25 square miles of shimmering ice fields, and in places is steep enough to put the fear of falling into nearly anyone. Clallam Indians, who mostly saw the mountain from a greater distance, just called it *P-Kowitz*, or "White Mountain."

As for the two lovely alpine lakes you'll be visiting, I'm afraid I would have fallen into the old habit of giving them one of those classic, sorely overworked mountain names—Heather Lakes, Diamond Lakes, Upper and Lower Looking Glass lakes, or something like that. Such titles seem to do a better job of leaping out at you when you're sitting in your kitchen on winter nights pouring over maps, dreaming of the North Cascades high country. But alas, these pockets of mountain water are known as the Bagley Lakes, named in honor of a heck of a good engineer and all-around nice guy on the Bellingham Bay and British Columbia Railroad.

Since we're on the subject of names, you may wonder about "Nooksack"—the name of the river you followed for much of the way to this trailhead. This was a name commonly used by early explorers for an Indian people who lived to the west, in the sunrise shadow of Mount Baker. *Nook* is roughly a word used to mean "people," while *sack* meant "fern," or specifically, the "bracken fern." Depending on how you choose to put it together, you end up with either "people of the bracken fern," or more commonly, "fern-eating people."

Bracken Fern

Before you assume that these people were either living in a place with a dull pantry, or else had palettes that were remarkably easy to please, you should perhaps take a closer look at just what the bracken fern has to offer. Though there is controversial evidence suggesting that bracken fern is actually toxic, the young "fiddlehead" stems it produces are quite delicious, offering a taste not unlike asparagus. The Nooksack practice of burning areas in the forest to encourage fern growth may have been inspired by a desire to bring in deer, which also like to feast on young bracken stems. But clearly, such activity had the added advantage of providing ferns for people too.

Natives weren't the only ones to make use of this most common of the American ferns. When times were tough during the Middle Ages, people pulverized the underground portion of bracken stems into flower for bread. Some American settlers, on the other hand, tried bracken as a treatment for worms.

Now that we've gotten our name tags on straight, let's head down the trail. The path winds down and then crosses the dam at the end of Lower Bagley Lake, at which point you can get down to some serious walking. Woven underneath wind-tousled branches of mountain hemlock are thick mats of huckleberry, false hellebore, and Sitka valerian, bistort, showy sedge—and, since this is the Heather Meadows area, plenty of red mountain heather. These mountain heathers aren't true heathers, like those found in Europe, but their dense, matlike growth and small, needlelike leaves are quite similar. When you come across a mat of heather, get down on your knees and take a close look at the exquisite urn-shaped flowers hanging off the plants—carefully crafted bells from some splendid fairy kingdom.

At 0.7 mile is an intersection at a stone arch bridge. The trail coming in from the left will take you either back to the parking lot, via the east side of Lower Bagley Lake, or up to the warming hut. Our walk continues straight, however, to the north side of Upper Bagley Lake. Keep your ears open here for the *eeek!* of the pika, or rock rabbit, which lives in the cold gray jumbles of talus that flank so many of these lush alpine meadows. At 1.1 miles you'll reach the fringe of Upper Bagley Lake, on the very edge of the 117,500-acre Mount Baker Wilderness. Although at this point you're only 0.75 mile from what in winter is a hustle-and-bustle ski area, this tiny alpine pocket, laced with cold water and braids of high country wildflowers, can truly seem a million miles away.

It was the famous British botanist David Douglas who, in 1827, first named these stunning mountains the Cascades, taking the title from the tumbling waters far to the south along the Columbia River. In time other names were tried, such as Snowy Mountains and the President's Range, but in the end it was Cascades that stuck. More than a century and a half later, that name strikes at the heart of American mountain lovers—not so much for the images of waterfalls and cascades it provides (though there are plenty), but for icy lakes and glacier-scoured cirques and basins.

WALK #25—HARTS PASS

DISTANCE: 2 miles

ENVIRONMENT: Mountain

LOCATION: Okanogan National Forest. From the town of Winthrop, drive west on State Highway 20 for approximately 8.2 miles. Just before a bridge, turn right onto Goat Creek Road, and follow this to the village of Mazama. (Do not cross back over to Highway 20 just before Mazama.) Continue up this road, past the end of the pavement at Lost River and into the national forest. Just past Ballard Campground, bear right and begin climbing a steep, narrow road to Harts Pass. Our walk begins from the pass (not at Slate Peak), heading north along the Pacific Crest National Scenic Trail. *Note:* Use special caution when traveling Harts Pass Road. Trailers are not allowed.

Though this walk is but a tiny slice of the magnificent, 3,000-mile-long Pacific Crest Trail, it's clearly the stuff of wild day-dreams. From the shoulders of Harts Pass the world explodes in mountains—a crisp, rugged collage of rock and timber and sky. Despite the long twists and turns required to get to the trailhead, all in all this is a gentle walk, easily managed by even young hikers.

The body of these mountains is a rich mix of metamorphic rock—quartz, marble, gneiss, and schist—that were squeezed and

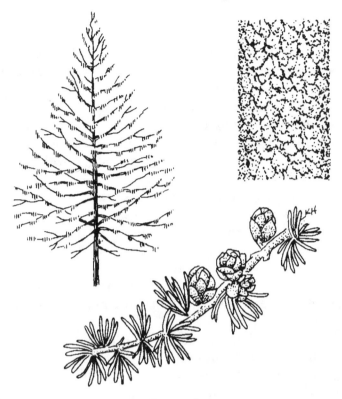

Tamarack

heated by magmas lying deep within the earth. In time, the land that forms the spine of the Coast and Cascade ranges—a ridge stretching from northern California into southern Alaska—heaved into the sky, in this particular area reaching a level roughly 8,000 feet above where it first began. Yet in the end, it wasn't grand swells of earth that gave the North Cascades their rugged, distinctive beauty. For that we can thank the long, cool centuries that gave rise to glaciers. At one point, all of western Washington, almost to Seattle, was covered by a vast sheet of ice, in places thousands of feet thick. The steep, knifelike ridges, the headwalls and amphitheaters, the grand "U"-shaped valleys like that of the Methow River far below you—all were carved by these tongues of ice.

The beginning of our walk meanders along a classic mix of coniferous forest, including tattered quilts of tamarack, framed to the east by wildflower meadows. Early on, the trail crosses a large talus slope, which in summer runs thick with the *eeek! eeek!* of the pika, or rock rabbit. Such cries of protest at being disturbed may seem overdone, but keep in mind that the pika has a lot of work to do. Before the short, sweet mountain summer comes to a close it will have to cut bushels and bushels of grass and leaves, lay them out carefully on the rocks to cure, and then store them away in its underground pantry for the coming winter.

This is a wonderful walk for flower lovers. There are no less than six dozen flowering plants in the immediate area, which makes this as fine an alpine garden as you'll find almost anywhere in the North Cascades. Watch for red heather, willow, phlox, yarrow, pussytoes, and white moss heather—the latter plant hung with exquisite bell-shaped white flowers.

The view at our turnaround point—a small saddle reached at 1 mile—can only be described as glorious. To the west are saw-toothed ridges, steep, scoured ravines, and polished headwalls—all blending together to form the rugged eastern fringe of North Cascades National Park. The lower reaches of the slopes are wrapped in spruce and fir, but as you move upslope these yield to the tenacious tamarack.

As you make your way back down the trail, notice the fire tower to the north, atop Slate Peak. This is one of many such towers throughout the Cascades. For decades, lookouts have been used as a means of early fire detection; at the height of their popularity, there were 93 in the North Cascades alone. One of these, named Desolation, was where Jack Kerouac came to spend a lonesome summer of writing.

Back in the 1930s, when the chief of fire control for the state of Washington heard that the Russians were doing mass parachute jumps, it dawned on him that this might be a perfect means for fighting forest fires. He wrote off to Moscow for information, had it translated, and before long was conducting experiments dropping sand bags—and later, men—into the meadows and forests surrounding Winthrop. (This little experiment, by the way, is what gave birth to American military paratroopers.) One of these early firefighters, a man by the name of Francis Lufkin, got into smoke jumping for practical reasons; the wage of $191 a month was $56 more than he could make on the ground. Lufkin admits that the whole idea was hard for the old rangers to accept. "We had quite a job selling smoke jumping," he says. "They used to think we were nuts."

WALK #26—RAINY LAKE

DISTANCE: 2.2 miles

ENVIRONMENT: Mountain

LOCATION: Okanogan National Forest. Take State Highway 20 (North Cascades Highway) east out of Rockport or west out of Twisp to Rainy Pass. Turn south onto Forest Road 500 and follow it for 0.1 mile to the Rainy Lake trailhead and picnic area. Rainy Lake is handicapped accessible.

There's no getting around the fact that unless you walk the trail to Rainy Lake early or late in the day or during the off-season, you're going to have company. But because this lovely trail is paved and level, it's perfect for those who aren't able to navigate difficult paths. What's more, the lake itself is splendid—a tiny jewel set in the vast green and gray folds of the high Cascades.

Before entering the spruce-fir forest, a place of trunks and branches wrapped in thick cloaks of lace lichen, you'll pass nice smatterings of both horsetail and false hellebore. This latter plant can be easily recognized by its veined leaves and tall stem, which at this altitude reaches a height of about 3 to 4 feet. The range of uses for false hellebore is amazing. Alkaloids in the plant have been used for centuries to lower blood pressure and heart rate. And if you're a gardener, you may recognize the name "hellebore" as a type of insecticide; that insecticide is this plant, dried and ground into a fine powder.

Also growing in the area are nice clusters of lupine, rue anemone, and pearly everlasting, which you've probably seen time and again in dried flower arrangements. Rising from all this vegetation on the far side of the North Cascades Highway, is the rugged flank of 7,790-foot Whistler Mountain. Some historians suggest that, rather than being named for a person, Whistler takes its title from the hoary marmots living there. The habit these fat, furry vegetarians have of emitting a shrill whistle whenever danger approaches has earned them the nickname of whistle-pig. Hoary marmots often make their homes in jumbles of rocks high in the mountains, where the weather allows them to be active only a few months out of the year.

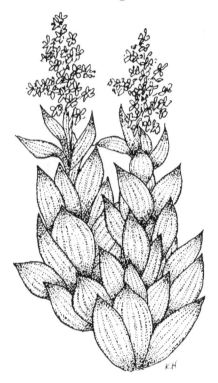

False Hellebore

At 1 mile, the thick curtain of forest begins to ease and the first glimpses of Rainy Lake appear in the distance. Before you actually reach the lakeshore, however, take note at 1.1 miles of the beautiful ribbon of ferns on either side of the trail, which at one point courses down the hillside ravine like a great green river. Ferns of all types were widely used by Indian peoples throughout the Northwest—the fronds as liners and coverings, and the roots and young "fiddleheads" as food. In medieval times, many Europeans believed that ferns bore a single golden flower which bloomed only on Midsummer's Eve. Anyone lucky enough to find the flower was assured riches beyond their wildest dreams.

Rainy Lake is a classic Cascade alpine lake, right down to the rugged glacial headwall carved out by Lyall Glacier. While serious glacial sculpting and scouring took place during the ice age of 12,000 to 20,000 years ago, many of the glaciers here in the Cascade high country managed to gain some additional muscle during another, mini–ice age that occurred just 3,000 years back. No matter how massive they get, glaciers don't exactly barrel down the mountain like some kind of ice-bound freight train. Their work—which has been nothing less than to shape virtually every dramatic cirque, horn, or "U"-shaped valley you see before you today—is a slow, patient business, usually involving movement of no more than several feet per day.

WALK #27—BRIDGE CREEK

DISTANCE:	2.8 miles
ENVIRONMENT:	Mountain
LOCATION:	Okanogan National Forest. Head west from the town of Winthrop on State Highway 20. The parking area for our walk is located on the right (north) side of the highway, just west of mile marker 159. The trail takes off directly across from the parking lot, on the south side of the highway.

If you love the mountains, it's virtually impossible to drive the North Cascades Highway without feeling an itch to get out and do a little walking. The perfect cure lies along the Pacific Crest Trail, at Bridge Creek. Admittedly, you'll have to contend with a little highway noise for the first half-mile or so. But soon thereafter the trail enters a world marked by the cool, almost ethereal silence of a mature spruce-fir forest, punctuated here and there by the whisper of streams as they dance down the mountain toward Lake Chelan.

This is a wonderful walk for familiarizing yourself with some of the more common plants of the high Cascades. Within the first 0.25 mile of trail you'll pass silver fir, Engelmann spruce, grand fir, willow, huckleberry, and trailing rhubus, along with a nice mix of wildflowers. The diversity of vegetation here is in large part thanks to the crest of the Cascade Range, which always manages to wring great quantities of snow and rain from the bellies of the clouds. After passing this divide, the clouds descend into warmer air; because warm air is able to hold on to more moisture, less ends up falling as rain or snow.

When I walked this trail, there were thousands of spider web strands across the trail, flying in the first light of day like so many silk threads. Such web strands are formed from a protein-based liquid spiders draw out of their undersides. When the critter no longer needs one of the lines it has cast, it simply eats the line, thus "recycling" valuable material.

At 1 mile into the walk you'll intersect connector trails to Copper Creek and Stiletto Peak. At this point you're just a mile away from North Cascades National Park, and less than 30 miles from beautiful Lake Chelan. If you've ever doubted the raw power of glacial ice to shape the high country, then Lake Chelan should convince you once and for all. The bowl of this lake, scooped out 20,000 years ago as if it were so much sherbet, is 50 miles long and a phenomenal 1,528 feet deep, which makes it the seventh deepest lake in the world. Lake Chelan basin is remote country. The population along its upper reaches is served not by road but by ferries, which make regular runs to Stehekin Landing to deliver groceries, clothing, and hardware.

Soon, dramatic views begin to open up to the southeast of the rugged Cascade crest, capped by the cold, ragged summits of Lincoln Butte, Twisp Mountain, and Hock Mountain. Just under 4 miles east of where you now stand, at a windswept saddle called Copper Pass, Alexander Ross became the first European to cross the roof of the Cascades in 1814. Ross had his share of grand times as a trapper for the Hudson's Bay Company, crisscrossing the vast reaches of the Columbia watershed in search of beaver. Unfortunately, after foolishly invoking the ire of the Snake Indians in what is now southern Idaho, Ross's men were robbed of all their goods. Ross himself was demoted, and not long afterward gave up the trapline to become a school teacher.

At 1.4 miles is an open slope, the airy views courtesy of an avalanche that steamrolled through here several years ago. The sudden addition of sunlight provides wonderful growing opportunities for plants that wouldn't be able to make it in the shade of the forest. Look here for alder, raspberry, red elderberry, lady fern, and Sitka mountain ash. This is our turnaround point, though you can certainly continue on, hitting the national park boundary in 0.6 mile.

WALK #28—CEDAR FALLS

DISTANCE: 4 miles
ENVIRONMENT: Forest
LOCATION: Okanogan National Forest. From the town
of Winthrop, head west on State Highway
20. At 0.5 mile past mile marker 176, turn
left (south) onto Forest Road 200. Follow
this for 1 mile, at which point it will dead-
end at the trailhead.

Being influenced to a degree by the "rain shadow" effect of the Cascades (the process whereby mountains block the advance of moisture), the Cedar Falls Trail is wrapped in a unique blend of dry and wet. There are both thin veils of timber, allowing nice views, as well as pockets of cedar cradling lush braids of creeks. This walk is the perfect antidote for road-weary travelers who find themselves struck with a sudden urge to chuck the camper and see what this country really looks like, from the inside out.

Our trek begins in a fairly open weave of ponderosa pine, Douglas fir, willow, and snowbrush. This latter plant, sporting thick, finely toothed evergreen leaves, takes its name from the fact that it grows in areas of heavy snow; the weight of the snow on the branches eventually leaves the plant with a permanent curve. Because it tends to grow in dense, almost impenetrable thickets, snowbrush is a favorite hiding place for deer.

Soon a nice view of the Methow Valley will appear over your left shoulder, backed by Goat Peak. The name Methow, first assigned to the river that runs from the high crest of the Cascades down to the Columbia, was taken from an Indian tribe that once lived on a wedge of land bordered by Lake Chelan and the Columbia River. These people had a rather more colorful name for the Columbia, calling it *buttlemuleemauch*, which is thought to have meant "salmon falls river."

Such view spots are eventually lost in dense forests, the bottom branches pruned by the trees themselves because they no longer have access to the sun. The sheer number of conifers growing in the West suggest that there must be definite advantages to the evergreen way of life. For starters, you don't have to expend energy each year to create new leaves—a real advantage when growing seasons are short and nutrients sparse. Second, when conditions are favorable for growth to occur—and that often happens outside of what we consider to be the standard growing season—these trees can make the most of it. Finally, conifers are well suited to the dry summers that mark so much of the West; not only can they store more water than hardwoods, but the waxy coating on their needles helps them conserve it. This isn't to suggest that hardwoods don't do well in certain niches. But their need for moderate summer temperatures and regular moisture isn't easy to satisfy. If a hardwood tries climbing the mountains to get more precipitation, it will find the climate too cold; if, on the other hand, it moves downslope to warm up, then conditions may be too dry. It's no wonder that in the Northwest the ratio of conifers to hardwood has been estimated at a thousand to one.

By 0.75 mile the textures along the trail have grown even more interesting. There are the soft drooping branches of western redcedar and bracken fern, and the furrowed cinnamon bark of ponderosa. There are shaggy braids of lichen dripping from the branches of the conifers, and soft green maple leaves rustling in the wind; frothy white blooms of ocean spray, and smooth green leaves of pipsissewa.

Cedar Falls waits for you at the 2-mile mark. This is a fine little double fall—a 15-foot drop split by a tongue of rock, and then another plunge of a dozen or so feet right below that. In fact, sitting on the large rock located between these two drops, you can enjoy the delight of stereo waterfalls. There are some beautiful cedars cradling this stream channel, as well as maple and black cottonwood. Also, look for a mammoth old Douglas fir nearby, on the trail side of the creek—a tree that probably started growing about the time the Pilgrims stepped off the Mayflower.

WALK #29—BEAVER LAKE

DISTANCE:	2.5 miles
ENVIRONMENT:	Forest
LOCATION:	Okanogan National Forest. From the town of Twisp, head east on State Highway 20 for approximately 12.5 miles. Just west of the Loup Loup Summit, turn north onto Forest Road 42. Follow this for 3.7 miles, then turn left onto Forest Road 4235. Stay on Forest Road 4235 for 1.6 miles to Forest Road 4235100. Follow Road 4235100 for 2 miles to the trailhead. *Note:* This trailhead is easy to miss; watch closely for a small sign on the right side of the road marking trail 356.

The longer you poke around the rugged peaks dividing the Okanogan and Methow river valleys, the more the place seems to pull you in. There's plenty of beauty here—mountains clad in yarrow, syringa, paintbrush, balsamroot, and sagebrush, framed on either side by valleys that in spring are filled with apple blossoms. There's also some fanciful history to be found in this area, as labels like Happy Hill and Fuzzy Canyon suggest. Perhaps the most intriguing of these old monikers is Loup Loup, a name you already encountered on a highway summit leading to this walk.

Loup is French for wolf, and it was the name given by French and Canadian fur trappers to a nearby stream. Why it ended up Loup Loup, instead of just Loup, is anyone's guess. Personally, I have this image of a trapper running out of the woods with his pants around his knees, yelling "Loup! Loup!" as he bolts by his astonished friends. At any rate, the tag was later tacked onto a silver-mining area just east of here. The town boomed during the 1890s, but then faded into oblivion as the price of silver took a nosedive.

Just north of the old town of Loup Loup is the site of another mining town, called Ruby. Ruby was a mecca for seamy adventurers of all kinds—a fact that led one writer to call it "the Babylon of Washington Territory." In the late 1800s one of Ruby's leading citizens had a tidy enterprise of rustling his neighbors' cattle and then selling the meat in his downtown butcher shop. One night the local cattlemen rode into town carrying a long rope with the butcher's name on it; fortunately, some of the man's drinking buddies stopped the execution by promising a trial. The cattlemen placed the butcher under heavy guard, but alas, the guards got drunk and the butcher hightailed it for the hills. (It's easy to see how part-time Methow Valley resident Owen Wister wouldn't have had to look far to find good characters for his book, *The Virginian*.)

As this area was logged not long ago, the first part of our walk passes through a fairly homogeneous forest of young lodgepole with a few hemlocks and white pines, lightly sprinkled with buffaloberry, strawberry, and whortleberry. On the left at about 0.2 mile you can see a giant tamarack and a Douglas fir that somehow escaped the saw. The latter tree is surrounded by splendid mats of kinnikinnick. This was a popular ingredient in smoking blends of Native Americans across the continent (in the West it was often mixed with the bark of red-osier dogwood), while herbalists around the world swore by kinnikinnick as a diuretic. The rather strange-sounding common name, which means "smoking mixture," actually originated among the Algonquian Indians of the East, and was carried here by French Canadian fur trappers.

At 0.6 mile is a split in the trail; stay left. As you continue to climb, at 1 mile you'll be afforded a fine view of the Cascade Mountains rising off to the west. Most of the moisture that drifts in from the Pacific is snagged by this range; the peaks you're in now wring out most of what's left, leaving the country immediately to the east high and dry. Besides this "rain shadow" effect, there are two other factors that influence the amount of moisture in any given place. The first is elevation. The higher you go, the cooler it gets. Cool temperatures not only induce additional precipitation, but they also reduce the rate at which moisture is lost from evaporation. In a similar vein, the plants you see growing on south slopes under the full slap of the sun will often be much different than what grows on shadier, cooler north faces.

Beaver Lake is reached at 1.25 miles. This is a delightful little water pocket, rimmed by a rather nice weave of spruce, fir-pine, and alder. If you look at a national forest map you'll note that there are actually many landforms in this area with the name "beaver" attached to them—an indication that this was once prime fur trapping country. For a time, the local Indians called Concully Valley east of here *Sklow Outiman*, which means "money hole." The name arose from trappers dropping into the valley, nabbing a beaver or two, and then using them as currency at nearby Fort Okanogan.

▪ OREGON ▪

OREGON

· · ·

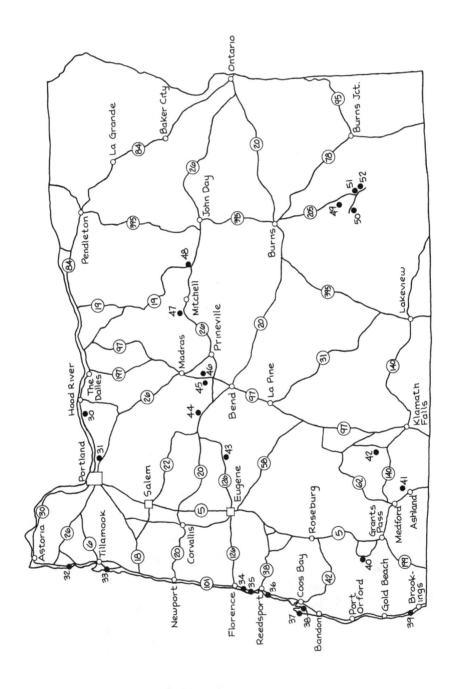

Western Oregon

WALK #30—GORGE TRAIL 400

DISTANCE:	2.8 miles
ENVIRONMENT:	Forest
LOCATION:	Columbia Gorge National Scenic Area. Located along Interstate 84, approximately 50 miles east of Portland. Heading east or west on I-84, take exit 51, and follow the signs for the U.S. Forest Service's Wyeth Campground. Follow the signs for the trailhead, which is located on the south side of the campground.

If you're the kind of walker who's dead set against any sort of traffic noise, then this trail may not be your cup of tea. On the other hand, no walk in this part of the Columbia Gorge is faster to get to, nor allows such uncrowded, easy walking. The Gorge Trail 400 is a perfect family leg-stretcher, an ace to play when you're sick and tired of watching the world hurtle past your windshield at 65 miles per hour.

Just 0.1 mile down the path, you'll come to a fork in the trail; turn right and cross a wooden bridge over Gorton Creek. This stream, named in honor of Edwin Gorton, who homesteaded here in the 1890s, is framed by a rich grove of Douglas fir, with a few broadleaf maples, western redcedar, and vine maples tossed in for good measure. If you've been out and about farther upstream in the Gorge, say around The Dalles, it will be clear right from the start that this is a place with far more moisture to spend. Within the 80 miles of the Columbia Gorge is an incredible range of precipitation: Wind River, just across the Gorge and slightly downstream from where you're walking, receives an impressive 100 inches of rain per year, while The Dalles gets a meager 14 inches. Add to this the striking elevation changes on both the north and south sides of the river, and you end up with a region that offers nearly every kind of northwest habitat your heart could desire.

Our path climbs gently around a north-facing hillside, meandering past gardens of pathfinder (also called silver green, because of striking color differences on each side of the leaves), as well as twisted stalk, false Solomon's seal, and star-flowered Solomon's seal. Telling these latter three plants apart can be somewhat of a challenge at first, since all wear shiny, ribbed leaves. But twisted stalk does indeed have a zigzag to it, and in May and June its cream-colored flowers will be found hanging down one to a stem. False Solomon's seal, on the other hand, flies its tiny blooms in a dense cluster at the top of the plant. And finally, star-flowered Solomon's seal wears its star-shaped flowers in a loose arrangement along the top of a 1- to 2-foot-tall stem. As summer progresses, all three of these plants will gain beautiful red berries.

At 0.4 mile is the first of several talus slopes along this trail—steep runs of broken basalt, in places wrapped in the soft, velvety heads of various mosses. This is also a good place for clear views across the Columbia River, toward the stark, steep dome of Wind Mountain. As you can almost guess by looking, Wind Mountain has more than its share of rock slides, nearly all of which end up rumbling across Washington State Highway 14; in fact, the upper layer of Wind Mountain is said to be heading south at a rate of about 40 to 50 feet every year. Just downstream from Wind Mountain is the Cascade Slide—granddaddy of them all. Long ago the Cascade Slide rolled clear across the Columbia, damming it for a short time until the river pushed through, leaving in its wake a jumble of rocks that caused enormous problems for early navigators. Lewis and Clark made note of the numerous dead trees lining the banks in the area—each one a casualty of the river having been temporarily impounded. Analyzing samples of these trees through radiocarbon dating, scientists were able to determine that the Cascade Slide occurred sometime in the 13th century.

It's for good reason that so many slides occur on the north side of the Columbia. Rocks covering the top of the uplands are comprised of a volcanic basalt which, as it cooled, became riddled with vertical fractures. Each year moisture leaks through these cracks, soaking the layers of ancient soil underneath. Those ancient soils, in turn, rest on another kind of basalt, which for all practical purposes is impermeable. Sooner or later the saturated soil gives way, sliding down the face of the older rocks like an oiled plate on a tilted table.

Our path stays more or less level, passing through beautiful groves of Douglas fir, broken here and there by the bright lavender flower heads of rosy plectitis, as well as ever more impressive runs of talus. Our final talus slope is reached at about 1.3 miles—a vast blanket of rocks, framed at the head by sheer towers and domes of gray basalt. This is the perfect place to hear the *eeek! eeek!* of pikas, a pleasant little rodent that looks rather like a guinea pig with a rabbit's face. Because pikas don't hibernate, in cold climates they spend the summers harvesting leaves and grasses and laying them out to cure on flat rocks; this "hay" is then stored in underground chambers for winter dining.

Our turnaround is just 0.1 mile past this enormous talus slope, beside a lovely, moss-laden stream. Bird-watchers will want to watch for brown creepers, white-breasted nuthatches, western flycatchers, and ruby-crowned kinglets.

If someone in your group doesn't feel much like walking, try to twist their arm into driving west on Herman Creek Road (the road that runs past the campground), picking you up at the Herman Creek Work Center, which is reached via this trail about a mile and a half west of our turnaround.

WALK #31—SANDY RIVER

DISTANCE: 1.3 miles

ENVIRONMENT: Forest

LOCATION: Oxbow Regional Park, 20 miles east of Portland. From Interstate 84, take exit 18, and follow the signs for roughly 12 miles to Oxbow Park. (Keep alert for these signs, as the route is full of twists and turns.) Once inside the park, take the main road east as far as you can go. The end of this road is marked by a one-way loop, running counterclockwise. As you turn into the back side of the loop you'll see one large parking area on your right, followed by a smaller parking area, located beside a couple of outhouses. Our parking area is the third one on the right, just past these outhouses. In the woods beyond the parking area is a sign that says "River Access, Group Camp;" our path begins by descending a set of stairs. *Note:* Please remember that pets are not allowed within the boundaries of the park. In addition, a vehicle entry fee is charged to help defray park operation and maintenance costs.

Oxbow Regional Park is a remarkable resource—yet another prize in a region whose people have long made parks, gardens, and natural areas priorities in their lives. There aren't many frustrations that a long, slow walk along the Sandy River won't ease, few problems that won't fade in the face of these rich forests and trailside runs of wildflowers. If you enjoy this walk, keep in mind that Oxbow Park has about 14 more miles of trail waiting for you to explore.

At the bottom of a long set of stairs is an intersection; turn left, and in 0.1 mile you'll reach another junction, this one marked with the letter "M." We'll turn right here, following a path that cradles the Sandy River around the edge of a large peninsula. This beautiful watercourse has worn a number of name tags over the past 200 years. When one of Vancouver's explorers stumbled across it in the fall of 1792, he named it Barings River, more than likely in deference to a wealthy English family of financiers. Thirteen years later, Lewis and Clark would remark that the river reminded them of the Platte. "The river throws out large quantities of sand and is very shallow," they wrote. In the end the pair decided to call this the "Quicksand River," a name that stuck for nearly 50 years.

Whatever you call it, though, few will fail to notice its charms—weaving and dancing past rocky floodplains, slipping past islands dotted with shimmering groves of willow and black cottonwood. Besides being a corridor for bird travel, the Sandy also provides critical spawning grounds for coho, fall and spring chinook, and winter and summer steelhead. If while on this walk you find yourself hungry for a closer look at the river, stay clear of steep banks, where currents run deep and fast. Instead, follow one of several spike trails that meander out onto the floodplains. When you get there, keep an eye peeled for osprey, merganser, and dippers.

In those moments when your attention isn't on the river, it will probably be on an engaging mix of trailside trees and plants. Look for western redcedar, grand fir, Pacific yew, salal, sword fern, horsetail, thimbleberry, vine maple, false Solomon's seal, twisted stalk, red huckleberry, low Oregon grape, trillium, strawberry, spirea, and, at roughly 0.25 mile, a fair amount of miner's lettuce. Miner's lettuce is distinguished by a stem poking through the center of a pair of leaves that form a saucer near the top of the plant. A somewhat similar plant, Siberian miner's lettuce, sporting leaf pairs in a more traditional shape, can be found about 0.5 mile farther down the trail, just past Group Camp Two shelter. Despite wearing popular names alluding to miners, these tasty items from nature's pantry were actually introduced to newcomers by native people. (Please remember that all plants in the park are protected; no collecting is allowed.)

At 0.9 mile is an intersection marked with the letter "L." Turn right here, on a path thick with the shamrocklike Oregon oxalis, as well as nice patches of bleeding heart, the blooms of which you may recognize from your local flower shop or nursery. On any given spring or summer day this is also a great place to stop and cock an ear for the sounds of songbirds. The performers will likely include the song sparrow, Townsend's solitaire, Swainson's thrush, Wilson's warbler, robin, Bewick's wren, and, if you're lucky, the secretive black-headed grosbeak. Just 0.2 mile from this last intersection you'll reach junction "J," where a trail comes from behind and to the right. Continue straight for another 0.1 mile to an unmarked intersection. Turn right, and follow this path back to the loop road where you left your car.

WALK #32—OSWALD WEST STATE PARK

DISTANCE: 1.3 miles
ENVIRONMENT: Coast
LOCATION: This trail takes off from the northernmost
■   parking area in Oswald West State Park,
■   which is located on the west side of U.S.
■   Highway 101, 4.3 miles north of Manzanita.

Oswald West State Park is a delight from stem to stern—for campers, for picnickers, and most certainly for walkers. While on any summer day or pleasant off-season weekend it may take you a half-mile to fully escape the sound of cars reeling down Highway 101, the visual beauty of Oswald West starts with the very first step. The trail begins with a lazy traverse of a hillside thick with spruce, below which can be heard the tumbling sound of Short Sand Creek—at this point very nearly finished with its headlong dash to the sea. As you walk this stretch of pathway, keep your eyes open for the bushy fronds of sword ferns, as well as the ivory, lemon, and lavender of fringe cups, Oregon oxalis, and yellow violets. According to one legend, the world's first violets were created when Cupid made the mistake of telling his mother, Venus, that a group of young girls were more beautiful than she was. Enraged, Venus began bludgeoning the girls until they turned blue and shriveled into violets. These unlucky girls, then, were the first "shrinking violets."

This coniferous forest is also a good place to watch for pine siskins, a small finch easily spotted in the pine, spruce, and alder groves found along much of this coast. Besides being a bit of an acrobat when it comes to feeding—often hanging upside down to pluck seeds—pine siskins are also extremely sociable birds; if you see one, you'll probably see many. Since they are somewhat drab in color, one of the best ways to spot pine siskins is to look for yellow patches on their wings visible during flight. You'll also probably see Steller's jays here—those raucous panhandlers that seem to have made a profession out of working the nearby picnic area.

At 0.5 mile the trail forks; stay left. Soon after this junction you'll be afforded fine coastal vistas, including one of lovely Short Sand Beach, which is framed by a ragged curtain of Sitka spruce. Just after a small observation point, the trail begins winding gently

Pine Siskin

Steller's Jay

downward, reaching at 0.75 mile a lovely beachside picnic area—as idyllic a lunch spot as you could hope to find.

Rather than returning the same way you came, follow the pathway around to the southeast side of the picnic grounds, where a paved walkway leads up to the south side of Short Sand Creek. The abundant moisture in this little ravine makes for a wonderful variety of plant life, including salmonberry, monkeyflower, bleeding heart (which you may recognize from your favorite garden shop), alder, skunk cabbage, salal, and devil's club. Salal, with its thick, green leaves and pale pink, bell-shaped flowers, often forms vast, almost impenetrable patches of vegetation along the Oregon coast. The berries of salal are quite tasty, not altogether unlike a blueberry, and were an important food source for coastal Indians. As often as not the berries were crushed and dried into small cakes, which were later dipped in whale or seal oil. David Douglas, the noted botanist who "discovered" the salal plant in 1825, took it back to Europe and tried without success to turn it into a commercial fruit crop.

The devil's club you see growing along the creek warrants a little caution. These sharp spines growing out of the stems of the plant made it the curse of early Northwest explorers, especially when you consider that for some the scratches caused troublesome allergic reactions. Devil's club was not entirely without redeeming qualities, however. Some native peoples claim to have used it successfully to treat mild cases of diabetes, and the juice of the berries was reportedly a good remedy for lice.

When you reach the footbridge at 0.85 mile, turn around for a moment and savor the view downstream—Short Sand Creek dancing down lush, green banks toward a jumble of driftwood, and behind that, the frothy, broken white lines of the ocean waves rolling forever into shore. At 0.9 mile is another trail junction, where you'll turn left. Follow this for just under 0.4 mile back to Highway 101.

If you live in landlocked environs as I do, where the sea is far, far away, then you're likely to find Oswald West State Park the perfect coastal daydream—something to cherish long after you've left this magical shore.

> For all at last returns to the sea—to Oceanus,
> the ocean river, like the ever-flowing stream of
> time, the beginning and the end.
>   —*Rachel Carson*

WALK #33—CAPE TRAIL

DISTANCE: 5 miles
ENVIRONMENT: Coast
LOCATION: Cape Lookout State Park. From the town of
Tillamook, head west on 3rd Street, and at
the edge of town turn south onto Three
Capes Scenic Drive. Cape Lookout State
Park is about 12 miles south of Tillamook;
our trailhead is located approximately 2.5
miles south of the park entrance.

Cape Lookout is one of the largest capes in the state of Oregon. Anchored to the lush foothills of the Coast Range, it forms a windswept, 400-foot-high tail of basalt that runs for nearly 2 miles into the sea—a kind of final exclamation point before the continent yields to 64 million square miles of Pacific Ocean.

Actually, Cape Lookout isn't really Cape Lookout at all. Explorer John Meares gave that name to another cape 10 miles to the north, but chart makers in the middle of the 19th century inadvertently applied it to this more prominent landform. Before long the mistake was well entrenched in the minds of mariners, who doubtless would not have taken kindly to "fixing" something as important as a navigational chart merely for the sake of historical accuracy. In the end, maybe John Meares would have been mollified, since cartographers eventually decided to name his original Cape Lookout "Cape Meares."

This walk begins in a grove of young to middle-aged Sitka spruce. You could roam the entire North American continent and never find a more thoroughly useful and magnificent tree than the Sitka. In the right conditions, such as can be found on Washington's Olympic Peninsula, or along the misty islands of British Columbia and southeast Alaska, the Sitka grows at phenomenal rates, sometimes reaching a height of 200 feet in the roll of a single century. It's a stately tree, with a straight trunk and a top of sweeping, tightly needled branches rising in gentle arcs toward the sky.

And yet, what has long pulled Americans toward the Sitka is not beauty, but usefulness. The tree has a clear, consistent grain, and the highest strength-to-weight ratio of any wood in the world;

Black-capped Chickadee

Salmonberry

pound for pound, it's every bit as tough as steel. This made it the wood of choice for, among other things, the props, wing beams, and ribs of World War I airplanes—many of which came from spruce cut from Oregon and Washington forests. On a more peaceful note, Sitka spruce has long been used for violin and piano sounding boards; in fact, it's roughly equivalent to the even-grained, elastic Norway spruce, which for centuries has been the preferred material of some of Europe's greatest instrument makers.

Some of this popularity the Sitka spruce could have done without. Today only a tiny fraction of the great trees remain, which isn't too surprising when you consider that even 50 years ago Sitka was being harvested in Oregon and Washington at a rate of nearly 250 million board feet per year—more than 10 times the optimum regrowth rate. Written in 1950 about the high cuts of Sitka on national forest lands, botanist Donald Peattie's words still ring true: "The spruce in the national forests constitutes a national reserve which could meet a national emergency. But it should not, in the judgment of the conservative, be called on to help out private industry just because the lumber and pulping companies are running short. They will have to solve their own problems and bring into line the rate of cut with the rate of natural reproduction."

Besides Sitka spruce, by 0.5 mile the trail is cradled by a number of beautiful western hemlocks, and the ground peppered with redwood sorrel, wild lily-of-the-valley, sword fern, and salal. As you walk through this forest, keep your ears open for the melodic songs of chickadees, rushes, and warblers, which on calm mornings drip like sweetener from the branches of conifers. In all the diverse habitats of Cape Lookout State Park, ranging from marsh and beach to headland and forest, there are more than 150 species of birds, including a number of sea ducks and passerines.

At just over 0.5 mile into the walk the timber on your left will open up, offering magnificent views to the south of Cape Kiwanda and Nestucca Spit. To the west is the blue wash of the Pacific, yawning into the haze of the far horizon. In the next mile you'll begin to spot growths of box blueberry and salmonberry—the latter a 3- to 10-foot-high shrub with leaves composed of three double-toothed leaflets. The pink flowers of this shrub, visible from March to July, are exquisite. Indian peoples of the region treasured both the fruit of the salmonberry, which they sometimes mixed with fish oil, and the young peeled shoots. The bark was also used to make a saltwater tea, which some say was effective in easing labor pains.

By 1.5 miles the trail levels out nicely, offering in the more open sections some wonderful views both to the south and of Netarts Bay and Cape Meares to the north. At just over 2.6 miles, you'll reach the tip of the cape, a grassy, windblown promontory.

Cape Lookout is the perfect place for whale-watching. Its elevation gives you an extended view, and shallow-water whales tend to pass by very close to the point. If you do decide to try your

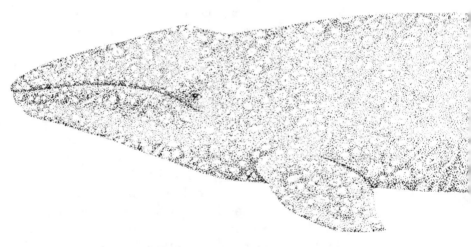

Gray Whale

hand at spotting these grand creatures, try to get here early in the morning, before winds whip the surface of the sea into whitecaps; also, morning light can help illuminate the whales as they surface and blow. (Alternatively, overcast skies will eliminate the problem of glare.) Gray whales have an uneven, splotchy color about them, with ridges along the back just forward of the tail. A whale with a tall dorsal fin and a striking black-and-white color pattern is a killer whale, a species often seen in groups. And finally, those with large, square-shaped heads and wrinkled-looking skin, blowing water at about a 45-degree angle, are sperm whales.

WALK #34—WAXMYRTLE TRAIL

DISTANCE: 1.7 miles
ENVIRONMENT: Coast
LOCATION: Oregon Dunes National Recreation Area, Siuslaw National Forest. From Florence, head south on U.S. Highway 101. In about 8 miles, turn right (west) at mile marker 198, following the signs for Siltcoos Beach. One mile from this junction you'll see the Stagecoach Trailhead on the left (south) side of the road. Park here. To reach Waxmyrtle Trail, follow a footpath that runs along the south side of the road you came in on, until you reach the entrance road into Waxmyrtle Campground. Cross the bridge over the Siltcoos River, and immediately take a right.

Waxmyrtle Trail, a slow, beautiful meander along the elevated southern banks of the Siltcoos River, is one of three pathways in this area sometimes referred to as "Stagecoach Trails." The name speaks of a time before the 1920s, when travelers would roll up and down the hard pack beaches during low tide on their way to and from the towns of Florence, Coos Bay, and Reedsport. And a cushy Cadillac-of-a-ride it was, at least compared to the rocky, rutted roads that most stagecoach passengers had to endure! Our walk begins near the point where stages crossed the Siltcoos River.

As noted, to reach the Waxmyrtle Trail you must work your way up the footpath that parallels the entrance road, and then cross a bridge to the south side of the Siltcoos River. This trail is not in any hurry to reach the ocean. The path winds to and fro, gently rising and falling along the twists and turns of the Siltcoos River, taking you either through or very near some fine forest, estuary, deflation plain, and foredune environments. This is the perfect walk not only to clear some of the Highway 101 traffic noise out of your head, but also to acquaint yourself with several of the more common plants and birds of the Oregon coast. (Consider that there are nearly 250 species of birds to be seen here, including over 100 kinds of song birds!)

Great Blue Heron

As you settle into the forested portion of Waxmyrtle Trail, you'll find yourself surrounded by a lovely weave of broom, salal, Sitka spruce, false lily-of-the-valley, bracken fern, red-flower currant, evergreen huckleberry, lodgepole pine (commonly referred to as shore pine), ocean spray, black twinberry, and, of course, western waxmyrtle. Waxmyrtle is a delightful little evergreen tree that produces wax-coated berries early in the fall. If waxmyrtle's other name, bayberry, sounds like something right out of a fragrance shop, it should; starting way back with the New England colonists, people have long boiled the berries from several varieties of this plant to create scented candles.

At just over 0.3 mile you'll come to an open, grass-covered bench overlooking the Siltcoos River. To the west lies the Pacific, waves gliding in for smooth landings on a long, flat line of golden sand. Directly across from where you're standing, on the north side of the Siltcoos, is a wonderful estuary habitat. If you've never had the pleasure of seeing a great blue heron feeding before, this is a good place to look. Though we tend to think of these hauntingly beautiful birds as residents of wetland environments, that's hardly where they spend all their time. They build large stick nests high in the canopies of trees, commonly using cottonwoods, alders, and Douglas firs. In the spring you can watch adult birds making trip after trip from their tree-top nests to their fishing grounds, and then back again, trying to keep up with the growing appetites of their chicks. The effort involved in such food shuttling is nothing to sneeze at, especially when you consider that great blue herons sometimes nest 20 or even 30 miles from their feeding grounds!

By 0.6 mile the trail has descended to river level again, beginning a trek through a medley of sandy hummocks and foredunes. As you walk this stretch, keep your eyes open for mats of purple pea, as well as beach grass, yellow lupine, and coast strawberry. Flying overhead, east of the foredunes, will be ospreys, northern harriers, and, during spring migration, a tundra swan or two en route to their breeding grounds in Alaska and the Canadian Arctic. From March 15 to September 15 you may run into closure signs near the mouth of the river. This is part of a concerted effort by the National Recreation Area and the Oregon Department of Fish and Wildlife to protect the endangered snowy plover during its breeding season. The eggs of the snowy plover, much like the adult bird itself, blend remarkably well into the scrapes of dry sand.

Visitors not only tend to scare the parents off the nest, but may accidentally step on the eggs.

If you spend much time on this, or virtually any other of Oregon's magnificent beaches, sooner or later you may find what's commonly referred to as a "drift bottle." These are glass bottles weighted at the bottom (pop, wine, and beer bottles are often used), cast into the sea by researchers so that they might better understand the movements of ocean currents. Each of these bottles will have a special return card in it, which you should fill out and mail back as instructed. Besides helping the researcher who launched the bottle, you'll probably receive information telling you when and where the bottle was first set adrift. Serious beachcombers have collections of drift bottles, some of which were launched from as far away as Russia and Japan.

WALK #35—TAHKENITCH DUNES TRAIL

DISTANCE: 4 miles
ENVIRONMENT: Coast
LOCATION: Oregon Dunes National Recreation Area, Siuslaw National Forest. From the town of Florence, head south on U.S. Highway 101 for about 13 miles, and then turn right into the Tahkenitch Campground. (The turnoff for this campground is 0.6 mile south of mile marker 203.) Once in the campground, follow the loop road to a parking area near campsite 30. Our trail takes off from here.

To walk from Tahkenitch Campground out to the mouth of Tahkenitch Creek is to capture the essence of the Oregon Dunes National Recreation Area. Here you'll see dark coniferous forests, the curling yellow crests of shifting dunes, and the pale flush of trillium, as well as the shout of ocean waves. While not a particularly difficult hike as far as the terrain is concerned, there's a substantial amount of sand walking involved—an activity that will tax you far more than any stroll down a typical forest pathway.

The first portion of this trail is usually thick with a steady drone of traffic from Highway 101. After a junction at 0.25 mile, though, where you'll head to the right, the traffic quickly fades and the rush of wind and the lilt of birdsong begin to take over. In no time at all you'll find yourself wrapped in a thick cloak of western hemlock, Sitka spruce, grand fir, and Douglas fir, with an under-story of salal, evergreen huckleberry, and rhododendron. This latter plant, incidentally, will in May produce clusters of pale pink flowers that are arguably as beautiful as those of any shrub in America. For all their beauty, though, the leaves and blooms of rhododendrons are poisonous, and honey made from their flowers is toxic as well.

At about 0.75 mile you'll reach the edge of a hill offering splendid views to the west. Immediately in front of you is a series of oblique and parabolic dunes. These are framed in back by a thin strip of lodgepole (shore pine), then a line of much smaller foredunes, and finally, the mighty Pacific itself. Sand is initially carried to this shore in the arms of ocean waves—the result of coastal rivers dumping sand into the sea, as well as waves constantly grinding down the sandstone from coastal headlands.

Longshore currents move these grains of sand generally southward, while high tides and waves then bring them onto shore. Once they dry, prevailing winds take over. Any wind over about 11 or 12 miles per hour is enough to make the sand grains begin to dance. Each grain typically moves only a few inches at a time, hopping over things that are hard, coming to rest when it reaches a soft surface, like that of a dune. Dune sculpting is influenced a great deal by seasonal winds, which blow out of the northwest in summer and the southwest in winter. The stronger winter winds give the basic shape to dunes, while the summer blows tend to form sharp cross-ridges. Driven by these seasonal blows, dunes actually migrate toward the northeast at a rate of anywhere from 5 to 15 feet per year.

The reason that the dunes are so expansive in this particular region is that this is one of the few places along the coast where prevailing winds can transport sand grains inland—in some places, for up to 2.5 miles—without having them intercepted by high cliffs and ridges. As a result, this has become the largest dune-covered coastal plain on the entire West coast, and certainly one of the most dramatic in the country.

Shortly after you gain this ocean vista you'll find a series of posts just to the south, forming a line that heads straight for the beach. These are trail markers. They will take you across the dunes, past the "deflation plain" (a place where winds have scoured the sands out down to the water table), and finally to the east bank of Tahkenitch Creek. From here you can stroll up and down the beach as you wish, lulled into the finest of stupors by the hiss of ocean waves. (Do be aware that from March 15 to September 15 you'll find closed areas near the mouth of Tahkenitch Creek; this is to protect the breeding grounds of the endangered snowy plover.)

WALK #36—UMPQUA DUNES

DISTANCE: 5 miles
ENVIRONMENT: Coast
LOCATION: Oregon Dunes National Recreation Area, Siuslaw National Forest. From Reedsport, head south on U.S. Highway 101 for approximately 8 miles. Go 0.25 mile past mile marker 222, and turn right (west), following the signs for North Eel Campground. Our trailhead takes off from the back side of the north campground loop, approximately 0.4 mile from the junction of the campground entrance road with Highway 101.

The Walrus and the Carpenter
were walking close at hand:
They wept like anything to see
Such quantities of sand:
"If this were only cleared away,"
They said, "it would be grand!"

"If seven maids with seven mops
Swept it for half a year,
Do you suppose," the Walrus said,
"That they could get it clear?"
"I doubt it," said the Carpenter,
And shed a bitter tear.

—*Lewis Carroll*
The Walrus and the Carpenter

If the Walrus and the Carpenter were that easily upset by "quantities of sand," they can count themselves lucky that they never set eyes on the Umpqua Dunes. These are the highest, broadest dune fields in all of Oregon Dunes National Recreation Area—4 square miles of golden troughs and rippled ridges that, at least when you're in the middle of them, can absolutely overwhelm you. Rising as high as 400 feet, these dunes are the childhood vision of an Arabian sand desert come to life; a line of mangy, squawking camels making their way along a nearby cornice would hardly seem out of place.

Our walk begins through a short stretch of coniferous forest, the understory thick with waxmyrtle, salal, evergreen huckleberry, broom, and rhododendron. When in bloom, the rhododendron growing in the ravine on your right is especially beautiful—tufts of pink petals floating on leathery green leaves. At 0.1 mile is a pathway coming in from the right; stay left. (This is about 50 yards past an intersection with a stairway heading uphill on your left.) The area around this latter junction is also a good place to get a close-up look at the crooked, reddish-orange limbs and evergreen

Salal

leaves of hairy manzanita. Soon you'll find yourself on the edge of the great dunescape—an ocean of sand piled into a graceful collection of rippled hummocks, ridges, and soft yellow valleys.

Because the volume of drifting sand makes it impossible to put marker posts here, those interested in walking the entire distance to the ocean should first climb to the top of the highest dune for a better look at the lay of the land. Gazing to the west, you'll see a tree island, not far from the ocean itself. Your plan should be to head to the northern edge of this tree island, at which point you'll pick up a line of trail posts running to the north. Follow these for a short distance, and then cross over the "deflation plain" to the beach itself. This deflation plain—an area where the sand has been scoured away by the wind down to the water table—is an entirely different world than that which lies on either side of it. Here the land is thick with rushes, sedges, willows, and silverweed, as well as an abundance of birds and small mammals.

Perhaps a word of caution is in order here. It's easy to become disoriented when crossing this vast expanse of dunes, and what was supposed to be a short walk can turn into a rather unsettling afternoon of aimless wandering. The trickiest part of the trek is not making it out to the ocean, but making it back. As you head out, you should pay close attention to what the scene looks like behind you. There are, for example, a couple of liquid storage tanks visible to the east on the other side of Highway 101 that you could "aim" for on your return trip. If all this sounds like more of an adventure than you're up for, know that you can still have a delightful time just ambling around the edge of this dunescape, never getting far from the lovely fringes of the transition forest.

WALK #37—SHORE ACRES STATE PARK

DISTANCE: 2.2 miles
ENVIRONMENT: Coast
LOCATION: Our trailhead is located approximately 3.6 miles west of Charleston on Cape Arago Highway. To find the beginning of the walk, continue just past the entrance to Sunset Bay State Park Campground, to a small parking area on the right side of the road. (This pull-off will be adjacent to a sign that says "Oregon State Park Botanical Garden 1/2 mile.") Our walk takes off from the parking area, along the Oregon Coast Trail.

If time allows for only one short walk along the Oregon coast, it would be hard to imagine a better one than this. First is an easy stroll along a particularly wild, jagged edge of the continent; then this section of the Oregon Coast Trail brings you to the heavily manicured, nevertheless magnificent site of the old Simpson Estate. Even though the great Simpson homes are no longer here, it doesn't take much imagination to see why during the first quarter of the 20th century this was considered to be the finest estate in all of Oregon.

At the beginning of the walk you'll pass fine clusters of salmonberry, which in April frame the path with striking splashes of scarlet blossoms. Early coastal peoples relied heavily not only on the berries of this plant for food, but also on the young shoots. As was the case for other kinds of edible plants, the tribes of the Northwest sometimes had individual family ownership of salmonberry patches; barring their destruction by fire or disease, these patches became sustainable food sources to be passed down from generation to generation. Another important food source for early peoples of the area was salal—a shrub sporting thick evergreen leaves and pink, bell-shaped flowers. In most places, the sheer abundance of salal made private ownership less of an issue than it was for salmonberry.

Fifty yards down the path you'll come to a junction; bear to the right, following the Oregon Coast Trail. At just under 0.2 mile is an overlook of a splendid little pocket beach framed on both

Steller's Sea Lion

Harbor Seal

sides by rugged headlands. Notice how the waves flow over these beautiful terraces, first submerging them and then gently pouring off their lips in thin, frothy veils.

Gray whales can sometimes be spotted during their fall migrations to calving and breeding grounds in Baja California, or during their spring swims to feeding grounds in the chilly waters of the Arctic. A mile south of this point, along a line of reefs that lie halfway between Shore Acres and Cape Arago, you stand a good chance of seeing harbor seals, elephant seals, and Steller's sea lions. The Steller's sea lion is an enormous mammal that takes its name from George Wilhelm Steller, who was the naturalist on Vitus Bering's great expedition to Alaska in 1740 to 1742. (You may recognize Steller's name from the Steller's jay—that large, raucous bird sporting a crest on its head, often seen flitting though the coniferous forests of the Northwest.)

Because the Steller's sea lion lacks a thick coat of underfur, it has never been popular with fur hunters. However, its habit of occasionally preying on squid, halibut, crabs, and other valuable species has hardly won it many friends among commercial fishermen. Sea lions breed in small colonies after what are often fierce battles between the males. Such conflicts are more than just staged events. In fact, it would be hard to find a single harem bull that doesn't wear more than a few scars around his neck from wounds inflicted by opponents' teeth. Pups are born singly, usually in June or early July; life remains perilous for several weeks afterward. Sometimes young are washed off the rocks by large waves and can't get back up again. Others are crushed by careless bulls, some of which weigh in at a whopping 2,000 pounds. Steller's sea lions do most of their feeding at night, along a band of ocean that extends roughly 10 to 15 miles out from the shore.

The trail continues to meander cliffside beneath growths of Sitka spruce and lodgepole pine, offering countless perches from which you can enjoy this wild, rugged coastline. At 0.5 mile, and again at 0.9 mile (near the more groomed portion of Shore Acres State Park), pay special attention to the tilted slabs of siltstone, sandstone, and shale that rise 30 to 40 feet out of the breakwater. The wind and storm patterns present along this stretch of coast during fall, winter, and early spring turn these slabs into launching ramps for incoming waves, sending them exploding in magnificent showers of glittery spray. Such surges are the forte of this wet, unbridled symphony—nature's equivalent to the crash of the symbols and the bellow of the brass.

At 1 mile you'll reach the groomed picnic grounds of Shore Acres State Park. A visitor podium stands near the cliff edge, and offers a wealth of interesting interpretive panels about the history of this splendid estate. Louis Simpson, son of timber and shipping magnate Asa Mead Simpson, came across this place early in the 20th century while out cruising for commercial timber. He fell in love with it, and in time managed to buy it from the owner, who was somewhat down on his luck at the time, for the paltry sum of $4,000. Over the years two separate mansions were built here. They sported magnificent entry halls, bedrooms, gymnasiums, and a 75-foot-long Roman bath complete with freshwater and seawater—both of which came hot or cold.

Portions of the Simpson Estate were often open to the public, especially the magnificent botanical gardens. As family fortunes began to wane, the property was eventually sold to the state, which razed the second mansion in 1948 because it could no longer afford the upkeep. Seven acres of the gardens, however, have been maintained in splendid fashion. Sixty different rose varieties can be seen here, 400 kinds of trees and shrubs, and 1,200 annuals. Approximately 1,000 bulbs are planted each spring. If you happen to miss the blooming season, don't worry. During the last three weeks of December the grounds are lighted and the garden house fully decorated for the holidays—a spectacular display of some 100,000 lights.

WALK #38—SOUTH SLOUGH SAMPLER

DISTANCE: 2.75 miles
ENVIRONMENT: Coast
LOCATION: South Slough National Estuarine Reserve.
From the town of Charleston, head west on
Cape Arago Highway for 0.1 mile, and turn
left onto Seven Devils Road. Continue south
on this road for about 4.3 miles, following
the signs for South Slough National Estuarine Reserve. Our walk begins on the Plant
Identification Trail, located behind the
reserve's visitor center.

South Slough National Estuarine Reserve, established in
1974, was the first national estuary in the United States; it is
without question one of the most engaging natural areas you'll find
anywhere in Oregon. Among these 5,000 acres are thick weaves of
plants growing in the upland forests, as well as a delightful variety
of birds on the salt marshes and tidal mudflats below. South Slough
is one of relatively few large, marine-dominated estuaries in this
country essentially unbroken by development. To date, more than
200 million acres of the world's estuaries have been lost, most of
them to the kind of "reclamation" that has consumed so much of
the rest of the Coos Bay estuary system to the north. (For a time the
town of Coos Bay was known as Marshfield, because it was built on
filled-in marsh.)

An estuary, in simplest terms, is a place where a freshwater
river joins the saltwater of the ocean. Largely because of a phenomenon known as the "detritus cycle," in which large amounts of
energy are made available through the decomposition of plants,
estuaries are unmatched when it comes to sheer quantity of food
produced. In fact, South Slough is more than five times as productive as a cultivated corn or wheat field, and seven times more
productive than the typical forest. This rich base of detritus, along
with an abundance of phytoplankton, creates a platform upon
which many larger, more familiar creatures can exist. We now know
that estuaries are crucial nurseries for literally millions of fish;
about 22 species of commercially harvested fish and shellfish are
found at South Slough alone. This area is also a wintering ground,

breeding area, or stopover point for hundreds of thousands of waterfowl. One of the more painful environmental lessons of this century has been that to destroy what at first might seem like a worthless patch of mud and marsh is to yank the threads from one of the most important webs of life on earth.

Our walk begins along the Ten Minute Trail (formerly the Plant Identification Trail), located behind the South Slough Visitor Center. This visitor center, by the way, is an excellent place to learn more about the intricate workings of estuaries. You can also pick up a small interpretive brochure highlighting some of the habitats you'll find along this walk. On the back side of the Ten Minute Trail is a small amphitheater; turn here on a side trail, following the signs toward Sloughside Pilings. The path will begin a steady descent through Port Orford cedar, red alder, evergreen huckleberry, and salal—that mix finally giving way to a cool, quiet slice of coniferous forest.

At 0.7 mile is a trail intersection. At this point we'll leave the main path, following instead a short side loop past a wall of salmonberry to a magnificent garden of skunk cabbage. Skunk cabbage, which is named for the fetid odor it gives off in spring when the large yellow flowers bloom, is perhaps nowhere bigger or more profuse than in this drainage. To me, this ravine seemed like some kind of wonderful fairyland—a place where you might expect to see newts and trolls standing on their tiptoes to better savor a bit of skunky perfume. One Northwest Indian legend claims that it was the skunk cabbage that brought salmon runs to residents of the coast. The grateful people rewarded it with a war club (the flower spike) and a fine blanket (the hooded bract around the spike). If you're here in the fall, look for places where the resident elk herd has come through, taking huge bites out of these plants.

At 0.8 mile you'll reach a lovely salt marsh, a mix of arrowgrass, pickleweed, and fleshy jaumea. At the edge of the marsh is a wooden platform from which you can get a wonderful view of some common feathered residents and visitors to South Slough. Be very quiet as you approach, and you may spot whimbrels, greater scaups, harlequin ducks, green-winged teals, wood ducks, great blue herons, common mergansers, cattle egrets, Brandt's cormorants, kestrels, yellowlegs, and, if you're lucky, even an osprey or a bald eagle. Besides being an important habitat for birds, salt marshes are also very effective as water purification systems. A salt marsh like this one can trap the sewage produced by thousands of homes, ultimately removing both nitrogen and phosphorous from the waste.

Continue north through "The Tunnel," which is an arched wall of hemlock, cedar, salal, and evergreen huckleberry; the line of dead Port Orford cedars you'll see along the way have been killed by root rot. At 1.25 miles intersect the main trail again near a rest room. Turn right, and follow the signs for Sloughside Pilings. Soon you'll find yourself on a narrow dike stretching into the water for about 0.1 mile before ending at a set of pilings. These pilings are the last remains of an old railroad trestle. The railway line was built to carry raw logs and then dump them into the slough; next they were tied together and towed in great rafts to mills located in nearby Marshfield and other points along the bay. Such logging activity actually drove most of the settlement at South Slough. Not only did the lands cleared by timbering lend themselves to settlers coming in and establishing farms, but the logging employees were a ready market for beef, milk, butter, eggs, and vegetables.

South Slough was established under the National Estuarine Reserve Research System. Under this program, scientists are to conduct intensive studies of several estuarine systems around the country, and then make their findings available to federal, state, and local policy makers. (One of the big problems with deciding how to manage these vital ecosystems is that we still know very little about them.) Though this system has not been without its share of problems, it remains one of the finest programs to come out of the federal hopper in many years.

WALK #39—INDIAN SANDS

DISTANCE: 0.6 mile
ENVIRONMENT: Coast
LOCATION: Samuel Boardman State Park. This walk takes off from a parking-picnic area along U.S. Highway 101 about 6 miles north of Brookings. You'll find the turnout on the west side of the highway, 0.5 mile north of mile marker 353.

The trail to Indian Sands drops like a shot off the busy Highway 101 corridor, leading you in just 0.2 mile to a weird, wonderful world of sand. Here are sandstone headlands and delicate dunes, sharply eroded cliffs and soft hummocks topped by purple beach pea and shaggy mats of shore pine. If you're in the market for aimless wandering, you can simply meander up and down a wonderful maze of convoluted escarpments and coulees. Alternatively, those in a more linear mood can pick up the Oregon Coast Trail at the point where you first come out into the sandscape—a route marked by a series of wooden posts with yellow bands.

True to its name, Indian Sands was visited by various coastal Indian tribes in both historic and prehistoric times. A great many arrow and spear points have been found, as well as various knives and scrapers—some of them from people who were living in and traveling through this area 8,000 years ago. It's rather astonishing to think that people were sitting here chipping points 1,000 years before the rise of the earliest known cities of Mesopotamia; the first exactly dated year in history, 4241 B.C., which was found recorded on an Egyptian calendar, was still nearly 2,000 years away!

The promontories of this area may have been especially attractive to early residents, since the presence of brisk winds would have kept troublesome insects at bay. Over time, though, those same winds eroded the promontories, pushing the cliff lines farther inland; thus, the farther away from the coast archaeologists explore, the more recent are the sites they find.

The people who lived along the Oregon coast in times past were well cared for by the bounty of both land and sea. There were a great many plants to be had, including an abundance of strawberries, blackberries, salmonberries, and huckleberries, not to mention ferns, skunk cabbage, and various seeds, greens, and nuts. Chinook salmon were taken along the coastal rivers in the summer, followed by coho salmon and steelhead trout. Perch, smelt, herring, and flounder were available in any season. While inland game animals were almost certainly abundant, it appears they never made up as much of the coastal Indian's diet as did fish.

While you're sitting here high above the ocean, it's fun to speculate about what really happened in this place. As you're wandering about the area, don't be surprised if you end up discovering a small piece of an arrow point or scraper lying in the soft, sandy hummocks and eroded ravines. If you do, examine it to your heart's content, but then put it back exactly where you found it. Researchers have launched significant archaeological investigations in this area; figuring out these cultural tales means having as many pieces of the puzzle in place as possible. This is why there's a law against collecting artifacts—a law that park officials are committed to enforcing.

WALK #40—ROGUE RIVER TRAIL

DISTANCE:	4 miles
ENVIRONMENT:	Mountain
LOCATION:	Bureau of Land Management. From Interstate 5, take exit 61, and head west toward the town of Merlin. In roughly 23 miles you'll reach a bridge crossing the Rogue River. On the north side of the river is the Grave Creek Boat Ramp; park here, and begin walking downstream on the Rogue River Trail. *Note:* Another trail parallels this one on the other side of the river. Because it traverses a cooler, more sheltered northern slope, it would be an especially good choice on a very hot day.

It would be hard to imagine a more staggering slice of riverscape than the Wild and Scenic Rogue. This is a watercourse with both peace and thunder running in its blood, a river perfectly matched to the mix of dramatic volcanic cliffs and quiet, forested niches rising from its banks. Boaters have long considered the Rogue from Grave Creek downstream to be a slice of heaven; it's hardly less appealing to those who love to walk.

French trappers were the first to use the term *rogue*—"coquin" in French—applying it to a group of Takelma Indians who were clearly unwilling to put out the welcome mat. Based on initial encounters the Takelma were long afterward described as a savage people, completely lacking in social or spiritual values—an attitude that grew by leaps and bounds when gold seekers began pouring into this region in the early 1800s. Of course, such judgments made it less unsettling when it came time to herd the Takelma onto reservations, where the people weakened and finally vanished altogether.

Most of the knowledge we have of the Takelma was gleaned by anthropologists, who, through conversations with the last of the elders, managed to piece together a sketchy, though intriguing picture of the culture. The lowland Takelma relied on salmon, deer, elk, rabbit, and birds for food, along with a wide variety of native grasses, fruits, nuts, leaves, and roots. Like other tribes, the

Takelma thoroughly loved a sport called "shinny," which was similar to field hockey, and played music on flutes made out of reeds from the wild parsnip. Major events in Takelma life, such as the spearing of the first spring-run salmon, acorn harvests, or successful hunting seasons, were marked with a variety of rituals and ceremonies of thanksgiving. Women were adept at weaving, tanning, and braiding, and made baskets of exceptional quality, including many that could hold boiling water. To a Takelma, being rich meant possessing such items as dentalia shells, flint, and, in some cases, pileated woodpecker feathers; such wealth, however, carried with it the responsibility of caring for less fortunate relatives.

Since we're dipping into history, you may wonder about the name Grave Creek, which joins the Rogue River near the start of our walk. In 1846 a young girl by the name of Martha Crowley, who was en route with her family from Missouri to the Willamette Valley, died and was buried here. When, two years later, a party of gold seekers on their way to California found the site desecrated, they gathered up the remains, reinterred them, and named this stream Grave Creek. Curiously, young Martha's death was only one of a long string of tragedies to strike the Crowley family. Martha's sister Matilda and her brother Calvin died along the Oregon Trail, as did Calvin's wife and child. Shortly after Martha's death here in Oregon, her father died too, just short of the fertile valley he had dreamed of for so long.

The first 0.5 mile of our path traverses open, sunny slopes sprinkled with cryptantha, Oregon sunshine, paintbrush, desert parsley, along with manzanita and canyon live oak. As you walk this stretch, notice the amazing difference in vegetation across the river, on the north-facing slopes; shielded from the sun, these hills have given rise to thicker, denser woodlands of alder, Douglas fir, Oregon ash, and rhododendron.

The first good opportunity for a break along the Rogue comes at 0.7 mile, where a side trail forks left and descends to the river. Just past this junction on the main path is a beautiful grove of canyon live oak, their twisted branches offering not only welcome shade, but a certain artistry and grace found in few other trees. Oddly, some live oaks—usually young ones—produce leaves with spiny margins, rather like a holly, while older trees tend to bear leaves with smooth margins; occasionally, a single twig will bear both. The strong, extremely durable wood of canyon live oak made it the perfect choice for making wagon axles and wheels, as well as splitting mauls.

A mile into the walk you'll cross a small seep, followed by a hill rich with a plant with succulent rosettes of basal leaves, tinged with red; in late spring to early summer it will also bear pale yellow flowers. This is sedum, a name derived from the Latin verb "to sit"—a reference to the fact that the plant grows very low to the ground. This is also a good place to see patches of Siskiyou iris.

The trail continues weaving through a mix of open areas and sheltered forests, arriving in 1.9 miles at a fork in the trail. You'll take the left branch down to the river, through a forest of ponderosa pine, Douglas fir, white oak, bigleaf maple, and canyon live oak. Though you'll have no trouble hearing Raine Falls, getting much of a look at it will require making a healthy jaunt downstream. (The trail on the other side of the river offers a much better view.) Raine Falls, which pours over an erosion-resistant slice of Rogue formation basalt, takes its name from a miner-turned-hermit who lived in a tiny cabin on the south side of the river. For a bed he used a web of old wires stretched in a corner of the room, covered with hay. Sadly, one day Mr. Raine decided he'd had enough of this world, and hung himself from the rafters of his woodshed.

WALK #41—GRIZZLY PEAK TRAIL

DISTANCE:	3.6 miles
ENVIRONMENT:	Mountain
LOCATION:	Bureau of Land Management. From Inter-state 5 at Ashland, head east at exit 14 for 0.6 mile to Dead Indian Memorial Road, and turn left (north). Travel for 6.6 miles, and turn left onto the Shale City Road. Follow this for 2.9 miles, turning left at a sign for Grizzly Peak Trail. Follow this for 0.8 mile, and turn left again; proceed for another 0.8 mile to the trailhead.

When the heat of summer begins pouring into the Rogue Valley, pushing temperatures toward the swelter mark, grab the binoculars and field guides and head for the cool coniferous forests of Grizzly Peak. Not only is this a splendid place to see wildflowers, but there are also stunning views, stretching all the way from California's Mount Shasta to mighty Mount McLoughlin in the Rogue River National Forest.

This peak is but one of many local natural features named after the great bear, *Ursus horriblus*, which from 1860 through the 1890s had quite a reputation for helping itself to steak dinners on the hoof. Though the grizzly is long gone from southern Oregon, I find it somehow comforting to think of a time when it thrived here—to imagine how each spring it would emerge from the den to roam this wild country, plucking fish from the streams, digging camas bulbs, wrestling the carcasses of winter-killed elk and deer from the lingering fields of snow.

Our trail begins in a forest of predominantly Douglas fir, sprinkled here and there with western redcedar and white fir. On the ground, look for strawberry, miner's lettuce, violet, lupine, trillium, and at 0.25 mile, an abundance of a very large plant known as bugbane. The genus name for bugbane is *Cimicifuga*, which is derived from a Latin noun for "insect," or "bug," combined with a verb that means "to put to flight." Much like hellebore, bugbane was used by native peoples to repel flies and mosquitoes.

In this same area you'll be afforded striking views to the northeast toward Howard Prairie (once known as Grizzly Prairie),

Mount McLoughlin, and the high, thickly forested country running north toward Crater Lake. Keep your eyes and ears open for the deep blue flash and boisterous call of Steller's jays, as well as the black hood and chestnut mantle of the Oregon junco. Energetic dispositions make both of these birds easy to see; in addition, the Oregon junco has a habit of feeding in relatively open areas. Also worth watching for are ruby- and golden-crowned kinglets, chickadees, brown creepers, and hairy and pileated woodpeckers.

The path continues to wind in and out of the forest, past nice clusters of red currant and snow queen, at 1.8 miles reaching a splendid promontory. Growing in and among these jumbles of rock is greenleaf manzanita; one look at the smooth, gnarled branches on the dead portions of these plants and you'll understand why in some places manzanita has long been known as "mountain driftwood." Here too is the succulent sedum, and in late April through May, the exquisite blooms of fawn lilies. At first, fawn lilies produce only a single leaf from a white, dog-tooth-shaped bulb. It's not until the following year, or even several years afterward, that a pair of leaves finally appears, along with a leafless stem bearing a single flower.

From this rocky perch you can look almost straight south to 5,910-foot Pilot Rock, which sits very near the California border; well beyond are the snowy flanks of 14,162-foot Mount Shasta. Slightly west of south is Mount Ashland, backed by the gentle rise and fall of the Marble Mountains. Those who aren't ready to call it quits can continue walking north on this trail toward the summit of Grizzly Peak, savoring more beautiful forests and yawning views along the way.

WALK #42—HEAVENLY TWIN LAKES

DISTANCE: 6.1 miles

ENVIRONMENT: Forest

LOCATION: Winema National Forest. From Klamath Falls, head west on State Highway 140. At about mile marker 41 you'll come to Forest Road 3651, which takes off on the right (north), toward Cold Springs Campground and trailhead. Our walk leaves from the campground-trailhead area, which is just over 10 miles north of Highway 140.

As far as I can tell, the fellow who named the natural features in this lovely slice of the Winema National Forest must have been on some kind of cosmic vision quest. The place we're bound for wears the striking name of Heavenly Twin Lakes, which, appropriately, lies just north of Imagination Peak. If you go north 5 miles you'll end up even farther out in the celestial sphere, this time at the feet of Venus and Jupiter peaks. (By contrast, the person in charge of naming in the region farther north was evidentally on somewhat more of a down-to-earth journey; his mountains are called Maude, Ethel, and Ruth.)

A walk across this gentle, forested plateau is perhaps best described not as a hike, but as a meditation. It's one of the best places in the area to work on Thoreau's notion of sauntering, to feel like Rudyard Kipling's cat, out "walking by his wild lone." In addition to a nice trailside mat of bleeding heart, twinflower, pipsissewa, whortleberry, and trillium, much of the forest itself is composed primarily of lodgepole pine, mountain hemlock, Engelmann spruce, and white pine. Since you'll be spending the next 6 miles with these natives, perhaps you should get to know a little bit more about them.

Engelmann spruce, which grows rather sporadically here, is a dark tree, lending a wonderful richness to the forest. It's the Engelmann you'll most often see huddled around the lakes of the high country, its straight spires poking into a thin blue sky. One of the Engelmann's more significant survival traits is that seedlings can hold their own in the shade of their parents, waiting patiently until they get a chance in the sun. Thus, barring fire, harvest, or

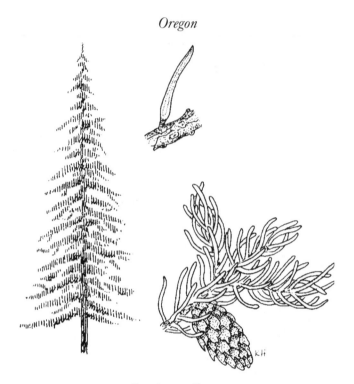

Engelmann Spruce

avalanche, a forest made up of Engelmann spruce will likely remain that way.

The mountain hemlock is one of the more graceful looking trees of this forest, with slender branches curving slightly downward in a gentle arc. Like the needles of its cousin the western hemlock, its needles are short—only 0.5 to 1 inch long. Unlike the western hemlock, however, here the needles spread on all sides of the twig, instead of in two rows. Also, the cones of the mountain hemlock may be 2 or even 3 inches long, whereas western hemlock cones are rarely much over an inch. As it climbs higher and higher into the mountains, where the climate is increasingly harsh, this tree becomes shorter and shorter. What was growing 100 feet high down in the moist lowland valleys will at timberline be little more than a prostrate shrub.

After walking along the Cold Spring Trail, you'll intersect the Sky Lakes Trail at 2.75 miles; bear to the right. A short distance later will be another intersection, this one with the Isherwood Trail; once again, keep right. If you want to add extra lakes to your trip with only about another 1.3 miles of walking, you can go left on the Isherwood Trail, which eventually loops around the north side of Heavenly Twin Lakes. At the next intersection you'd take a right, following Heavenly Twin along its east shore until you met up once again with the route for this walk. Whether you take this side trip or not, the main trek can be turned into a nice loop simply by returning to your car via the South Rock Creek Trail, which you'll find on the eastern edge of the Heavenly Twin Lakes.

On your right, soon after the intersection with the Sky Lakes Trail, is the small round basin of south Heavenly Twin Lake; this is followed soon thereafter by the north and much larger Heavenly Twin. This is a good place to watch for osprey as well as for the comings and goings of waterfowl. Right now these beautiful birds aren't nesting along the lakeshore, but a few do come fishing here from nesting areas 6 to 8 miles away. Unlike other birds of prey, the osprey eats nothing but fish; watching one hang high over a lake and then dive straight down to grab a trout with its talons is an extraordinary sight. Because pollutants tend to accumulate in the tissue of fish, osprey are hit hard when toxic chemicals enter the water system. The birds were on a rapid decline when DDT was still being used; the poison was altering the composition of their egg shells, causing them to break prematurely.

Sitting on the shore of this beautiful lake on a silvery autumn evening, a wedge of geese flying overhead bound for Klamath Lake, is to begin to feel that sense of sweet timelessness that so often rises from the heart of wild places. In certain moments you can almost feel akin to those French soldiers who were assigned the task of exploring the wilderness of the New World—an adventure task that 19th century historian Francis Parkman captures nicely:

> A boundless vision grows upon us; an untamed continent; vast wastes of forest verdure; mountains silent in primeval sleep; river, lake and glimmering pool; wilderness oceans mingling with the sky.

WALK #43—RAINBOW FALLS OVERLOOK

DISTANCE: 2.4 miles
ENVIRONMENT: Mountain
LOCATION: Willamette National Forest. From the town
of Eugene, head east on State Highway 126,
continuing past the town of Blue River. Turn
right (south) 0.7 mile east of mile marker 53
onto Foley Ridge Road, also known as Forest
Road 2643. Follow this for 6.4 miles, and bear
right onto Forest Road 460. This road ends at
our trailhead, in 0.3 mile.

Most people are too busy exploring the traditional approaches to Three Sisters Wilderness to give any attention to this small, out-of-the-way forest path. But if easy, uncrowded walking and breathtaking vistas are what you're after, this walk is sure to please. Although the first 0.4 mile of trail is through an old forest cut, the land has come back with bells on, and is today cloaked in a fine wash of willow, Oregon grape, starflower, fir, hemlock, cedar, bracken, and thimbleberry. Because there are really two forest communities here—one middle-aged and one fairly young—this is the perfect trek to get a feel for the changes that occur as a forest matures.

Two plants to watch for during the first 0.4 mile of the walk are snowbrush and thimbleberry. Snowbrush has shiny evergreen leaves with three main veins fanning outward from the stem. The underside is soft and hairy while the top is often gummy; hence another of the plant's common names—sticky laurel. When things begin to heat up around here in July and August, you may discover that the leaves of the snowbrush have curled along their center veins. This isn't a sign of ill health, but rather a nifty strategy for avoiding the drying effects of the sun. Elk and deer consider snowbrush to be a choice winter browse; if you're here after a rough winter, you'll see plenty of chewed stems.

Thimbleberry is another plant of note; at just under 0.4 mile it forms a hip-high wall of large, maplelike leaves. Curiously, though the plant's species name—*parviflorus*—means "small-flowered," its lovely white blooms often measure 1.5 inches across.

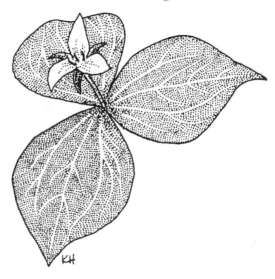

Western Trillium

In mid- to late summer thimbleberry sports lumpy, bright red berries; each of these "lumps" has developed independently from separate ovaries, coming together as they grow into what appears to be a single berry.

Soon you'll enter a mature forest of fir and hemlock. If you're here in June, off to your left will be the showy pink to purple blooms of red rhododendron, each perched atop a rosette of long, shiny evergreen leaves. Some people consider this the most beautiful shrub in the western United States—an accolade heartily endorsed by the state of Washington, which in 1949 made it the state flower. Rounding out the bloom parade are trillium, bedstraw, pathfinder, star-flowered Solomon's seal, three-leafed anemone, and, at about 0.6 mile, clumps of vine maple.

Before long, a rather striking canyon opens up on your right, the rim lined with a loose weave of firs spiked with Pacific madrone—the smooth, polished trunks of this latter tree rising like dancers caught in the middle of a delicate movement. The sculptor responsible for the canyon below is Separation Creek, which, although lost to view, can be heard making a mad dash to join the McKenzie River. The trail ends at our viewpoint, an absolutely magnificent perch along the northwest boundary of the Three Sisters Wilderness. Once you get to the overlook, carefully make your way to the southernmost rock outcropping, where you'll have a glorious view of Rainbow Falls to the west, as well as of North Sister, Husband, and South Sister peaks. (This mountain range is a real family affair; Brother, Wife, and Middle Sister peaks can be found nearby.)

PLEASE NOTE: This final stretch of path to the rock outcropping is narrow and steep; it is not a safe place for young children.

WALK #44—HEAD OF THE METOLIUS RIVER

DISTANCE: 0.4 mile
ENVIRONMENT: Forest
LOCATION: Deschutes National Forest. From the intersection of U.S. Highway 20 and Oregon State Road 22, head east on Highway 20 for 16.6 miles to a signed turnoff heading north along Forest Road 14, toward the Metolius River and Camp Sherman. (Coming from the east, Forest Road 14 is approximately 9 miles from the town of Sisters.) Follow this road 4.3 miles to the parking area and trailhead, on the left.

There was a time, so geologists say, when the waters of the Metolius ran not over the earth, but beneath it, in the dark, volcanic passageways that course through the feet of the great Cascades. Then the Green Ridge Fault began to shift and grind, pinching the underground waters upward until they burst forth as a full-fledged river—one that would ultimately give rise to a magnificent array of life. About 7 miles downstream from here, another, smaller spring system was created in similar fashion, and today feeds the Wizard Falls Fish Hatchery. The waters from that lower system pour from the earth at a year-round temperature of 50 degrees—perfect for the hatching and rearing of fish; in a single year up to 5 million eggs of six different fish species may be hatched at Wizard Falls.

Since the easy paved trail to the head of the Metolius River can at times be rather thick with people, you may want to take this walk either well off-season, or very early in the morning. Leave yourself enough time to really savor this special place. Even though

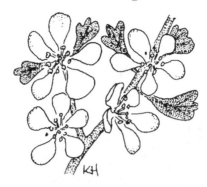

Bitterbrush

two other tributaries of the Deschutes River are also born from underground springs (Spring and Fall rivers), neither is as stunning as this one. To see the cold, clear waters of a large, fully formed river pouring out from a crack in the earth speaks to some deeply ingrained myth of plenty; the view immediately downstream, which includes pine-clad park lands and majestic, snow-capped Mount Jefferson, hardly diminishes the effect.

The name Metolius first appeared as "Mpto-ly-as" in a mid-19th century Pacific Railroad survey report. While there's some disagreement as to the exact meaning of the word, most scholars suggest that it refers to a light-colored salmon once found here. From the point where you now stand, the Metolius runs northward through ponderosa forests, makes a wide curve through a lovely canyon, and then ends its run with a quiet disappearing act into the slack waters of Lake Billy Chinook. All in all, few rivers pack more scenic punch per mile than this one.

The trail to the headwaters of the Metolius begins in a fine ponderosa forest, the understory spattered with tufts of manzanita and bitterbrush. Writing in his mammoth volume *A Natural History of Western Trees*, Donald Culross Peattie describes the look and the location of the ponderosa well. "Its shade is never too thin and never too dense," he explains. "Its boles and boughs frame many of the grandest views, of snow-capped cones, Indian-faced cliffs, nostalgic mesas, and all that brings the world to the West's wide door."

As is typical in coniferous forests, many of these ponderosa got their start thanks to chipmunks and squirrels that, in a fit of either absent-mindedness or over-preparation, left large caches of

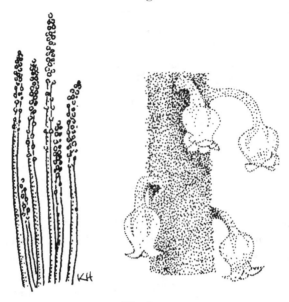

Pinedrops

the cones buried in the forests; pines in general have a higher sprouting rate when helped by busy paws than if simply left scattered on the surface of the ground. Because young ponderosa put most of their energy into establishing root systems, a 10-year-old tree may be only 1 or 2 feet high. Not until they reach the age of 15 or 20 will these trees really start putting on height or mass. This more rapid growth rate will continue for more than 100 years, and then slow to a crawl.

It's hard to think of another place where one feels more rewarded for just 0.2 mile of easy walking. The sight of this beautiful river emerging from the earth and beginning its gentle dance through the ponderosa is enough to rekindle our affinity for nature, to refresh our need to live in accord with the ancient rhythms of the earth.

> Here hills and vales, the woodland and the plain,
> Here earth and water seem to strive again,
> Not chaos-like together crushed and bruised,
> But, as the world, harmoniously confused:
> Where order in variety we see,
> And where, though all things different, all agree.
> —*Alexander Pope*

Central Oregon

WALK #45—SQUAW CREEK

DISTANCE: 5 miles
ENVIRONMENT: Desert
LOCATION: Crooked River National Grassland. Head north out of Redmond on U.S. Highway 97 for just under 6 miles, and turn left (west) onto Lower Bridge Road. Follow this for 11 miles, at which point you'll reach an intersection; the road going straight (north) is dirt, but you'll want to turn left (west), onto Holmes Road, which is paved. Follow Holmes Road for 2.2 miles, and then turn right onto Forest Road 6360. In about 5.1 miles you'll come to a "Y" intersection; stay left. In 1.5 miles, turn right onto Forest Road 6370. Follow this route for 1.6 miles to another "Y" intersection, this one with a gate. Park here, and walk down the left fork. (This is private land, so be sure to stay on the road.) *Note:* This route is not appropriate for low-clearance vehicles or those pulling trailers, or after heavy rains.

While the walk along Squaw Creek isn't exactly easy to get to, it's full of delightful sights and sounds. To drop out of the high desert on a hot summer day into a stream gorge layered with ponderosa pine, the rock walls ringing with the chortle of birdsong, is an experience not soon forgotten. Upon reaching the stream channel you can make a lazy meander downstream, traveling only as far as you like; this is, as writer Paul Klee put it, "a walk for a walk's sake."

From where you parked, the road continues beneath a power line, and soon thereafter drifts over the lip of a canyon rim and down to the east side of Squaw Creek. Fifteen miles to the west you can see the high, rugged weave of snowcapped cinder cones and lava shields that make up the central Cascades. These mountains routinely snag moist air running eastward from the coast— a catch that gives rise to thick, piney forests, and wonderful watercourses like the Metolius and Deschutes rivers, as well as Squaw Creek.

Our road descends through rabbitbrush, sage, rice grass, and yarrow, and at 1.25 miles passes through a lovely grove of mature juniper. The beautiful blue "berries" you see growing on junipers aren't really berries at all, but cones. While you may be familiar with the use of juniper cones to make gin, they're also used for other kinds of flavorings—in Germany for sauerkraut, in Sweden as a coffee substitute, and in France for certain kinds of beer. Juniper smoke, or incense, has long been used in sacred purification ceremonies by Indian peoples from Puget Sound to the Great Plains. Noting that lightning never seemed to strike juniper trees, Cheyenne Indians once burned juniper branches as a protection against the fury of prairie storms. The list of traditional medicinal applications for juniper is lengthy; even today the National Cancer Institute is studying certain species of this tree for use in the treatment of tumors.

At 1.3 miles the road comes to an end at an old campsite above Squaw Creek. From here you'll pick up a faint trail heading downstream, leading to a mix of open glens spiked with buttercups, as well as charming woodlands of alder, ponderosa, red-osier dogwood, and willow. Speaking of willow, between 1.5 and 1.7 miles it grows thick enough to make walking the trail somewhat difficult. Several places along Squaw Creek are lined with such thickets, comprised of either willow or alder, most watered by the cool springs that pour out from the base of the gorge. Keep plodding through, and you'll soon find yourself in an open park, much of it covered with the hollylike leaves of Oregon grape. (Oregon chose another, larger species of this plant—*Berberis aquifolium*—as its state flower.) Curiously, one of the alkaloids present in Oregon grape has the effect of stimulating involuntary muscles, which explains its use by some native peoples during childbirth to ease delivery of the placenta.

If you'd like to continue past this park, it will be easier if you cross over to the west side of Squaw Creek and resume your walk downstream from there. At 2.3 miles you'll come to one last alder-willow thicket. Pick your way carefully, and in 50 yards you'll find yourself in a vast open area, where the west wall of the gorge has been pushed back from the river channel. Those who make it to this amphitheater will find it a perfect place to rest, lunch, or simply contemplate the semidesert from the cool comfort of Squaw Creek.

WALK #46—CROOKED RIVER

DISTANCE: 2.4 miles
ENVIRONMENT: Desert
LOCATION: Smith Rock State Park. Head north out of Redmond on U.S. Highway 97 for approximately 6 miles, to the village of Terrebonne. Follow the signs eastward for 3 miles to Smith Rock State Park. Just after entering the park you'll see a climber-bivouac area and then a general parking area, both on the left. Continue past this second pullout for another 75 yards, to the next general parking area on the left. Our walk begins from here.

It must have been quite a sight. The air smelled of smoke and sulphur, and hot blizzards of red and gray ash poured down from the sky through the branches of alders, myrtle, and redwoods. Frightened "oreodonts"—short-legged browsing animals with long, blunt faces—bolted through the forest and across the meadows until they could run no more, their lungs and nostrils thick with debris. Though most of the falling ash had cooled by the time it reached the ground, on occasion there would come thick curtains of partially molten fallout. When these hit the earth they would hiss and steam, instantly solidifying into solid rock. It was this kind of deposit, later sculpted by wind, ice, and water, that created much of the dramatic weave of colored cliffs and ramparts that now line the Crooked River in Smith Rock State Park.

There are several stories to explain the identity of the "Smith" behind Smith Rock, though the most widely accepted tale isn't exactly a happy one. Camping here along the Crooked River in 1863 was a company of soldiers, which had been dispatched to show off American muscle to the local Indians. One of them, a chap named Smith, decided to climb up a promontory and have a look around. Unfortunately, no sooner had he reached the top when the boulder he was standing on gave way, and he fell to his death.

Today, arriving every summer morning at dawn, are hundreds of much better equipped, more sure-footed climbers than the hapless Mr. Smith. On most days you can see them working their way up the sheer, hard face of not only Smith Rock itself, but also the Monkey Face, the Dihedrals, Red Ryder Buttress, Picnic Lunch and Morning Glory walls, the Christian Brothers, the Monument, and Staender Ridge—3 splendid miles of rock face in all. Some say that this is the single best technical rock climbing site in the entire state.

While hanging hundreds of feet above the ground from a slab of tuff certainly has its appeal, our trek through Smith Rock will be a bit more mellow. From the parking area follow a paved walkway leading northwestward across the canyon rim, past a fine cloak of juniper, yarrow, sagebrush, buttercup, and yellowbell. In 0.1 mile is an overlook, offering wonderful views of not only the rugged rock and riverscape below, but off to the west, the snowcapped peaks of the mighty Cascades. Heading off from this overlook is a small dirt service road. Follow this sharply downward through juniper, ponderosa, and a smattering of red-osier dogwood, and almost before you know it, you'll find yourself in the arms of a beautiful valley.

In moist, sandy areas along the trail look for clusters of horsetail, which is a spindly, green plant with hollow, jointed stems and whorls of wiry branches. Like another kind of equisetum known as scouring rush, horsetail contains small amounts of abrasive silica, which made it useful to native peoples and settlers as a cleaning and polishing agent. Folk medicine recognized equisetum as a diuretic, and as recently as 100 years ago people were still using it to treat everything from kidney stones to dropsy. Interestingly, a Kootenai Indian legend tells us that it was the trickster Coyote who gave equisetum its distinctive stripes. Having fallen into the river during one of his pranks, after a great deal of struggling Coyote finally managed to grab hold of a scouring rush

Squaw Currant

growing along the river. Afraid that it would come out by its roots if he pulled too hard, he promised the plant that if it would hold fast, he'd reward it with a handsome decoration. The horsetail held, and Coyote kept his promise. Using clay and charcoal, he painted stripes up and down the stem, leaving the distinctive pattern you see today.

At 0.5 mile, after an enchanting walk beneath magnificent red-, chocolate-, and honey-colored spires and pinnacles, you'll reach a bridge over the Crooked River. Once on the other side, turn right, following the sign to Staender Ridge. From here you begin a lazy amble along the Crooked River, its channel cradled by rabbitbrush, mullein, currants, wild asparagus, and onions. At 0.7 mile you'll reach the first of several beaver-gnawed trees—this particular one a hearty juniper measuring a good 12 inches in diameter. Instead of building their lodges out in open water, here the beaver rely on tunnel and burrow systems dug into soft spots along the riverbank. The gnawed bark of juniper points to the beaver's remarkable ability to subsist on a variety of trees.

A hundred yards or so past this juniper is a fantastic old ponderosa with a makeshift bench—as idyllic a spot for daydreaming as you could hope to find. While native peoples in this region didn't relish the ponderosa as a food source the way they did some other conifers, they did occasionally eat the seeds, as well as the sweet inner bark. In fact, throughout central Oregon you can still

Beaver

find ponderosas with deep scars on the trucks from where local peoples peeled the bark for food.

In 1.2 miles you reach the turnaround point, adjacent to a lush braid of meadow and marsh filled with cattails and equisetum. This is a good spot to see red-winged blackbirds and kingfishers, as well as golden eagles soaring along the edges of the canyon rim. Roughly a mile-and-a-half downstream from this point is a pair of nesting prairie falcons. These are among the swiftest of the great fliers, capable of reaching speeds of nearly 150 miles per hour when diving on prey or defending their nesting areas. This defense of the nest, incidentally, is something that most falcons take very seriously, sometimes running off golden eagles twice their size. Falcons do not build nests of their own, preferring instead to lay their eggs on protected ledges, or occasionally in the nests of other birds.

WALK #47—CARROLL RIM TRAIL

DISTANCE:	1.5 miles
ENVIRONMENT:	Desert
LOCATION:	John Day Fossil Beds National Monument, Painted Hills Unit. The turnoff for the Painted Hills Unit of the monument is located on the north side of U.S. Highway 26, 3.8 miles west of Mitchell. Once you make the turn, proceed along the entrance road for 7.1 miles, following signs for the Painted Hills Overlook. The Carroll Rim Trail is located just opposite a turnout to the left that leads to the Painted Hills Overlook.

Those who manage to catch this trail on a sunny day at dusk, or shortly after dawn, are in for a treat. For it's then that these gentle swells and hummocks of mineral-bearing clay seem to come alive with color—a volcanic rainbow of black, bronze, green, buff, and crimson. Wind and water have been the master sculptors here. Over eons they carved into the heart of the John Day Formation, which consists of layer after layer of volcanic ash, deposited 30 million years ago from great eruptions in the ancestral Cascades. Within these layers (though not so much in the colorful painted hills) lie fossil treasures that have long captured the fancy of the world.

If we could turn the clock back 30 million years or so, the scene would look very different indeed. By then the wet rain forest of an even earlier time had slowly given way to a more temperate climate of about 40 inches of rain per year—a shift due in large part to the rise of the ancestral Cascade Range to the west. Much of the land was wrapped in a magnificent forest of alders, oaks, and dawn redwoods, as well as a collection of browsing animals, many of which would have looked far different from creatures of modern times. Today the fossil remains of this fanciful world—leaves and bones by the thousands—are found throughout the region.

A few miles to the west, in what's known as the Clarno Formation, is a place where you can find Oregon's beautiful state rock, the "thunder egg." A thunder egg is typically about the size and shape of a baseball, and the inside contains striking, colorful

Red-tailed Hawk

patchworks of quartz crystals and gray agate. Some geologists say that these internal patterns were formed as the result of expanding gasses, while others disagree, attributing them to the slow drying of a colloid or gel. Native myth, on the other hand, tells us that these were eggs of the powerful thunderbirds who lived in the high country. Thunder Spirits on Mount Hood and Mount Jefferson would routinely steal them from nests, and then hurl them at one another the midst of violent storms, which is how they ended up here in the lowlands. (Please remember that it's illegal to disturb or collect any geologic or fossil objects within the monument.)

The vegetation along the trail to Carroll Rim is fairly sparse, though each species lends a certain beauty to the dry skin of this semidesert landscape. The hills are softened by wavering clumps of bunchgrasses, including wheatgrass, fescues, and Indian rice grass, while blooms of prickly pear cactus, sage buttercups, salsify, yarrow, yellowbell, and sunflowers add welcome splashes of color.

The trail rises steadily, and in 0.5 mile you'll be among rugged cliffs and rimrock composed of a solidified volcanic material known as *ignimbrite*. In another 0.25 mile is the wooden bench that marks the end of our walk. From this windswept overlook you'll be afforded magnificent views to the south of a system of claystones known as the Painted Hills. More than two dozen elements blend together in various ways to give the Painted Hills their distinct colors; the yellows you see, for instance, are a mix of iron and magnesium oxides, while the rusty shades indicate the presence of iron oxide. Off to the southwest you'll see the juniper-laden Ochoco Mountains and the 17,000-acre Mill Creek Wilderness, near the northern edge of the Ochoco National Forest. (The word *Ochoco*, which may mean "willow," was first given to a fine little creek that runs through Crook and Wheeler counties. Some say the word was borrowed from a Paiute Indian Chief by that name, who lived west of where you now stand.)

This high perch is also a fine place to look for red-tailed hawks. It's a treat to watch these striking birds of prey soaring on hot summer winds, always on the lookout for small rodents scurrying across the ground below. In lightly forested areas redtails will be found conducting their hunts in more leisurely fashion, scanning the ground while perched in the top of the tallest tree. You may also want to keep your eyes open for golden eagles, turkey vultures, and prairie falcons.

WALK #48—BLUE BASIN OVERLOOK TRAIL

DISTANCE:	3 miles
ENVIRONMENT:	Desert
LOCATION:	John Day Fossil Beds National Monument, Sheep Rock Unit. From U.S. Highway 26, 33 miles east of Mitchell, turn north on State Highway 19. Approximately 2.3 miles from this junction, on the east side of the road, is the primary information center for the monument, and one of the best places to get a close-up look at fossils. Our trailhead is 3 miles farther north, also on the east side of the road. *Note:* Summer visitors should plan this walk for the early morning or late evening hours. Carry water.

Simply mention John Day Fossil Beds National Monument, and you're bound to light up the eyes of even the most jaded paleontologist. When it comes to the study of the Cenozoic era, which is roughly the 65 million years that stretch from the end of the dinosaurs to the beginning of the last ice age, this region holds what many scientists consider to be the most complete mammal fossil records in the world. Scattered throughout these dry hills are the fossils of saber-tooth cats and ancient rhinoceros. There are remains of an animal hardly bigger than a greyhound, which is ancestor to our modern-day horse, as well as giant boars, elephants, camels, horned gophers, tiny mouse-deer, and formidable-looking "bear-dogs." Toss in the wide range of plant fossils located here, which include everything from avocados and palms to redwoods and walnuts, and you can begin to sense the incredible richness of the place.

Beyond scientific value, however, there's also a striking beauty to this monument. The Sheep Rock Unit is a sharp, austere blend of blue sky and banded rock, split down the middle by the lazy green twists and turns of the John Day River Valley. At the high point of our walk, beneath the gnarled, pungent branches of an old juniper, you'll find a log bench overlooking a wonderland of cliffs, spires, and blue-green fossil beds. It's the perfect place from which to consider the 40-million-year-long climatic shift that

Big Sagebrush

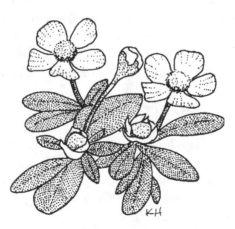

Sage Buttercup

pulled this country from a subtropical rain forest, to the high, windswept semidesert you see before you today.

The trail to Blue Basin Overlook begins with a gentle meander through a garden of big sagebrush and snakeweed, spiked with bluebunch wheatgrass, Indian rice grass, Idaho fescue, prairie stars, yellowbells, and sage buttercups. The gray-green tinge of big sagebrush is a common sight across most of the dry country that stretches from central Oregon southward through the far reaches of the Great Basin Desert. Although farmers who migrated into this region from the east looking to plant wheat or rye viewed big sage as nothing more than a nuisance—a hindrance to the plow—early Indian peoples had no such distaste for it. Several tribes made tea from the leaves to ward off colds and stomachaches (just thinking of the taste, which is truly horrible, would cure me), while others routinely collected the seeds of big sage and ground them into flour. Many Indians still burn sage leaves to purify their homes and sweat lodges.

In addition, big sage, which can live a hundred years, is extremely important to other plants and animals. Beneath its branches various grasses and wildflowers are protected from trampling and grazing. The lovely Indian paintbrush often obtains nutrients by tapping into the roots of sage. Western fence lizards and Nuttal's cottontails hide under the branches for both cooling and camouflage, while sage grouse dine on the bitter leaves. Big sage is also a good place to look for the sage sparrow—a 5-inch-long gray bird with a small black spot on the middle of its breast, and a white ring around its eyes.

You may notice that many of the sagebrush plants along the trail have large balls clinging to their branches. Each year various kinds of flies and wasps lay their eggs in the leaves and stems of the plants. In much the same way that human skin responds to insects bites, these plants often react to this irritation by swelling, forming these curious growths, or "galls." Once hatched, the insect larvae will feed on young plant tissue, eventually eating their way out of the gall.

Soon the trail begins to ascend, rising slowly past a parade of highly eroded pinnacles, spires, and amphitheaters of rust-red, chocolate-cream, and honey-brown. Smatterings of junipers appear, especially in the bottoms of washes protected from the hot blast of the desert sun. At 1 mile you'll hit the first of several steep

Mule Deer

sections of trail, though none lasts for very long. There's a fine bench to rest on at 1.1 mile, and another waiting at the high point, just 0.25 mile further down the path.

From the overlook you'll have the option of either returning the way you came, or continuing around the high knoll to the right down a slightly longer, though no less beautiful, pathway that eventually intersects the Islands in Time Nature Trail. At this junction, you'll turn left to get back to the parking lot. PLEASE NOTE: Some of this route is through private land; if it's to remain open to the public, hikers must stay on the designated trail. Less than 0.25 mile after leaving the high overlook on this alternative route, you'll come to the edge of a small draw sporting a beautiful stand of ponderosa pine. This stately little huddle of conifers has a way of taking the edge off the harshness of the surrounding terrain, especially if you happen to be here on a hot summer day. As you make your way past the braid of gullies and ravines leading to the John Day River Valley, watch the ground for coyote and mule deer tracks. Also, stop and look up once in a while; sooner or later you're bound to see a red-tailed hawk or an American kestrel skimming the skies high overhead.

Southeastern Oregon

WALK #49—KRUMBO RESERVOIR

DISTANCE: 1.5 miles
ENVIRONMENT: Desert
LOCATION: Malheur National Wildlife Refuge. From the town of Burns, head south for approximately 50 miles on State Highway 205, turning left (east) on a signed dirt road for Krumbo Reservoir. Our walk begins at the reservoir boat ramp, which is reached 4.3 miles from Highway 205. *Note:* This is a seasonal walk; the road into Krumbo Reservoir is closed from late fall to early spring in order to protect trumpeter swans.

Even though much of Malheur's sprawling 185,000 acres is closed to the public for the protection of its wildlife, the few access points available to visitors are wrapped in a weave of wild magic rivaling that found on any bird sanctuary in the United States. In the wake of melting ice in late February, the first movements of a virtual symphony of birds gets underway; northern pintails kick off the program, followed by tundra swans, Canada geese, lesser sandhill cranes, and white-fronted geese. The waterfowl migration reaches its crescendo in March, while migratory shorebirds such as willets, long-billed curlews, and avocets claim center stage during the month of April. By May the place is thick with yet another spectacle, this one featuring literally hundreds of thousands of songbirds. To date, more than 280 species of birds have been observed on the refuge, along with nearly 60 species of mammals.

The waters of Malheur are largely composed of snowmelt, carried here in the arms of the Donner und Blitzen and the Silvies rivers (at least in the years when agriculture doesn't suck the Silvies dry). Eight thousand years ago, when glacial melt was running

Sandhill Crane

down the mountains at full tilt, this entire basin was filled with water. Today, however, the water levels—and thus to some extent the number of birds—can vary from year to year. Though these marshes, meadows, and riparian zones have been key stopover and nesting areas for thousands of years, bird life was severely threatened around the turn of the century, when plume hunters came here by the dozens to kill swans, herons, grebes, and egrets (the egrets were wiped out altogether). A storm of national publicity, a fair amount of it generated by the Oregon Audubon Society, helped convince President Theodore Roosevelt to create a new federal Wildlife Refuge System, of which Malheur was a part.

If you're up on your French, you might wonder how such a beautiful place like Malheur ended up with a name that translates into "bad hour." For that tale we need to go all the way back to 1826. In February of that year, Hudson's Bay Company trapper Peter Skene Ogden was camped north of here, having stopped to recover a cache of furs and other goods. "We camped on River au Malheur," he wrote in his journal on February 14, "so called on account of property and furs having been hid here formerly, discovered and stolen by the natives." Thirty-three years later Captain H. D. Wallen of the Fourth Infantry had a herd of cattle bolt on him north of here, near the narrows, at which point he christened the water "Lake Stampede." Malheur, though, is the name that stuck.

From the boat ramp at Krumbo Reservoir head southeast on a faint path running along the shore. About the time this path begins to fade at 0.2 mile, look up to your right and you'll see a loose line of junipers on the slope above. Make your way up to these trees, which make a fine perch from which to survey activity on the reservoir. What you'll actually see here on any given day, of course, will vary greatly. In spring you'll find excellent waterfowl populations, including pintails, mallards, gadwalls, green-winged and common teals, western grebes, and coots. The beautiful tundra swan also passes through Krumbo in respectable numbers, and diving ducks like the redhead and canvasback will set up shop for the summer.

Though Krumbo is closed in late fall and winter, the activity at such times is impressive, primarily because this is one of the last places on the refuge to freeze. On some days as many as 2,000 Canada geese are here, as well as the beautiful trumpeter swan— a large bird with snowy white plumage and a black bill. This open

Trumpeter Swan

water is especially important to trumpeters because they don't migrate to warmer climates. In fact, there are times in winter when almost the entire Malheur population of trumpeters is right here on this reservoir. After teetering on the brink of total extinction, trumpeters were reintroduced to Malheur in the 1940s from a population at Montana's Red Rock lakes.

If you watch the south end of the reservoir you're likely to see both redhead and canvasback ducks diving down to dig starchy, nutritious sago pondweed tubors out of the mud. Other ducks may join in too, picking off insects that live among the leaves, as well as eating the "nutlets" that form as part of the plant's fruit.

When you're ready, continue walking on a faint trail heading southeast along the bench. Once past the open water of the reservoir, you can work your way down to a path along Krumbo Creek. There may be nesting coots, redheads, and canvasbacks in the bulrushes and cattails; try to give them as wide a birth as you can. The path continues east toward Krumbo Creek Canyon, and you can basically turn around wherever you please. If birds are your primary concern, you'll probably want to spend most of your time under those junipers you passed earlier, where in the soft light of dusk or dawn you can look down on some of the most enchanting bird life on earth.

Badger

WALK #50—PAGE SPRINGS

DISTANCE: 1.8 miles
ENVIRONMENT: Desert
LOCATION: Steens Mountain Recreation Lands. From the town of Frenchglen, located on State Road 205 approximately 61 miles south of Burns, head east on Steens Mountain Road. In 3 miles you'll come to the turnoff for Page Springs Campground; turn in, and follow it to a gravel parking area at the far southern end of the campground. Our walk leaves from here on a path that runs along the river, marked by a "Desert Trail" sign.

If thus far you've been reluctant to embrace the notion that deserts can be fabulous places, this walk will almost certainly change your mind. Here canyons of parched, ragged rimrock and vast swells of sage have been softened by the magic of a beautiful river—a long, winding ribbon flushed with shrubs and wildflowers.

The watercourse responsible for much of this life is the Donner und Blitzen, a National Wild and Scenic River. And no, it wasn't given that name because it drains the winter pasture of Santa's reindeer. One night during the Snake Indian War of 1864, troops under the command of Colonel George B. Currey were camped along these banks in a terrific rain storm. One of the soldiers was suddenly struck with the notion of christening the watercourse with the German words for thunder and lightning, and the rest is history.

The entire western flank of Steens Mountain was once part of a sprawling cattle empire, financed by Hugh Glenn and ultimately controlled by his son-in-law, Peter French. (Hence the name of the nearby village, Frenchglen.) Glenn was a wealthy farmer who controlled more than 50,000 acres of wheat land in California's Sacramento Valley; in the middle 1800s, those holdings made him one of the largest wheat barons on the continent. One year Glenn got the itch to sink his fingers into the cattle business. So he bankrolled Peter French, sending him north into the Harney country in 1872 with 1,200 head of cattle and six Mexican cowboys. Over the next 17 years French would create—

some say by illegal land swindles—a cattle empire of 45,000 animals running on nearly 200,000 acres of land.

Using lumber taken from the Blue Mountains 150 miles to the north, French built his outbuildings and corrals, as well as a stunning mansion for his wife. Apparently, though, her definition of "for better or worse" didn't include living on a ranch in the middle of nowhere; before long she divorced him and headed back to California, leaving him to his bovine dreams. Though at 5-feet 5-inches tall and 130 pounds Peter French hardly had much of a physical presence, more than a few Oregonians felt the sting of his ruthless ways. On the day after Christmas in 1897, one of French's neighbors decided he'd had quite enough of this little cattle king fencing off land that wasn't his, and shot him dead.

The walk follows the lazy meanders of the Donner und Blitzen River, the broad ribbon of grass, shrubs, and western juniper gradually narrowing as you make your way farther upstream into the river canyon. Along the way you'll see willow, thinleaf alder, Nebraska sedge, Kentucky bluegrass, scouring rush, reed canary grass, and red-osier dogwood. As for flowers, look for lots of beautiful monkeyflower, as well as lupine, salsify, and teasel. Teasel and salsify—both European introductions—have rather interesting backgrounds. Teasel is a coarse, weedy-looking plant 4 or 5 feet high, sporting spikes of light purple flowers; it's easily spotted 0.4 mile into the walk. In late summer large burrs form on the tops of teasel, which often persist until the following year. Settlers found that, when dried, the long, curving spines of these burrs were perfect for carding or "teasing" wool, hence its common name. (Its genus name, on the other hand—*Dipsacus*—comes from a Greek word meaning "thirst;" this is thought to be a reference to the fact that water accumulates in the cups formed by the base of the leaves.)

Salsify, on the other hand, is a plant with thick stems bearing bright yellow, dandelionlike flowers about 2 inches across. New England colonists brought salsify with them from Europe, where the roots had been used for centuries as food. Perhaps the best way to describe the taste of salsify root is to call it a blend of artichoke, parsnip, and oyster; this latter flavor led to another common name, oysterplant. (To make things even more confusing, in the East salsify is sometimes called noonflower, because the flowers tend to close up about that time of day.) Over time, many American Indian

Dipper

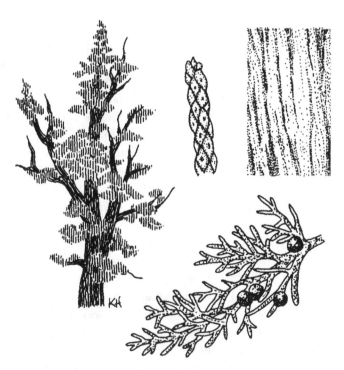

Western Juniper

peoples also adopted salsify as a food source; a few also used it to treat heartburn.

Continue up the canyon, past the songs of house finches, meadowlarks, bluebirds, robins, rock and house wrens, horned larks, and various types of sparrows. If you're lucky, you might also spot a dipper bobbing in and out of the Donner und Blitzen River. These rather plain-looking birds—one of John Muir's favorites— hunt for food on the bottoms of streams, sometimes walking partially submerged along the gravelly bottoms with wings held out at half-mast for balance. Dippers are a cheery bunch, singing merrily even in the middle of wind and rain and thunder. At 0.75 mile the trail makes a swing to the east. For about 0.1 mile it follows a canyon wall lined with the mud nests of swallows; they make quite a nice living here feeding off the large insect populations along the river. Just past the point where the river turns south again you'll cross a small stream that in most years you can jump over, and then another which you cannot. We're going to turn around at this second stream. If you haven't had enough, though, by all means carry on! The trail continues its riverside meander for many more miles, offering plenty of places to soak up a little magic—in a thick run of chest-high grass, by the cool quiet of a spring-fed pool, beneath the thick, knarled arms of a western juniper.

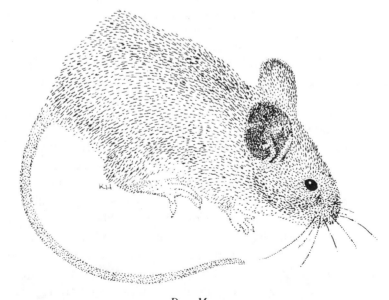

Deer Mouse

This fine walk along the Oregon High Desert National Recreation Trail was made possible because of tireless work by many people, including members of a national conservation and recreation group known as the Desert Trail Association. The Desert Trail is not just limited to the Oregon Desert; in fact, when completed it will stretch from border to border, winding through what are arguably some of the most engaging slices of desert in North America. Given the abuse and neglect of America's deserts in the past, the accomplishments of this group are a refreshing bit of progress in the long battle to preserve these precious ecosystems.

WALK #51—KIGER GORGE

DISTANCE: 1.2 miles
ENVIRONMENT: Mountain
LOCATION: Steens Mountain Recreation Lands. From the town of Frenchglen, south of Burns approximately 61 miles on State Highway 205, head east on Steens Mountain Road. In about 23 miles you'll come to a small road taking off to the left (north) to the Kiger Gorge Viewpoint. Follow this for 0.5 mile to the viewpoint, and begin your walk eastward along the rim of the gorge. *Note:* This is a seasonal road, closed in winter and spring.

If we're to better understand the creation of 9,773-foot Steens Mountain, then we'll have to turn back the pages of geology about 15 million years. At that time a great volcanic spew covered the area in ash and crystal-laden basalt to a depth of several thousand feet, rendering this entire corner of the state a flat, rather featureless plain. The Steens Mountain Uplift occurred 8 million years later, in a grinding collision between two large continental "plates" floating on the hot pudding of the inner earth. Basically, Steens Mountain rose, while the valleys on either side of it subsided. And finally, 10,000 to 20,000 years ago glaciers came on the scene; and to a large extent it was the work of glaciers, not uplift, that turned this mountain from something great, into something truly magnificent.

Though Steens is the only place in southeastern Oregon to have held glaciers during the last ice age, Kiger Gorge, on the northeast corner of the mountain, is easily one of the best examples of glaciation anywhere in the lower 48. There is an overwhelming depth and breadth to this curving, "U"-shaped valley—the kind of sculpting that would seem more fitting to a place like Norway, than to a lone mountain hanging above the Great Basin Desert. Nor is Kiger Gorge the only impressive chasm here; Little Blitzen, Little Indian, Big Indian, Wildhorse, and Little Wildhorse canyons are also well worth a close look.

Steens Mountain used to be known simply as Snow Mountain—a name it well deserves, considering that it's a rare year when you can make it all the way around the loop road before early July. The name of the mountain changed not long after Major Enoch Steens arrived on the scene in 1860, having arrived to develop a wagon road from nearby Lake Harney to Eugene City, located in the rich Willamette Valley to the west. One day while busy plotting his route, word came of an Indian attack against an army surveying party. Steens dropped his road-building project like a hot potato and headed east, where he established a fortified camp on Silver Creek, west of present-day Burns. Later that summer Steens had a row with a band of hostile Snake Indians, driving them up and over this mighty mountain; grateful miners and settlers referred to it as Steens Mountain from that time on.

Besides being a wonderful place for basking in the scenery, Steens Mountain is a botanist's dream. A phenomenal 600 species of plants have been found growing over a variety of life zones, including four that grow nowhere else (Davidson's pentstemon, Cusick's draba, Steens Mountain thistle, and Steens paintbrush). As you make your way east along the rim of Kiger Gorge, keep your eyes peeled for buttercups, yarrow, phlox, silky phacelia, milkvetch, needle-leafed sandwort, mat buckwheat, stonecrop, and pussytoes.

At a point about 0.2 mile from the parking area, you'll be able to look down on a beautiful lake at the head of Kiger Gorge; in the right light, and with a little wind blowing, it looks like a cache of precious gems. Also visible in the bottom of the gorge is the thin, silvery braid of water known as Kiger Creek. This stream dances northwest for more than 20 miles, not resting until it reaches Diamond Valley, just south of the parched volcanic domes of Diamond Craters.

Yarrow

Continue to follow the faint trail around the rim. In another 0.2 mile you'll have to make a jog around a large cut in the headwall. Our turnaround is at a small alpine water pocket lying just to the north of this jog. (Because of the very fragile nature of this environment, it's extremely important that you stay on the faint path already in place.)

No matter how out of place this mountain may seem, there's no getting around the fact that it represents the high country in all its glory—the brace of cold wind, the whistle of the marmot, the small pockets of snow shimmering under an August sun. The poet Byron once said that "high mountains are a feeling." Standing atop a place like Steens, you wish that feeling would never end.

WALK #52—EAST RIM VIEWPOINT

DISTANCE: 2 miles
ENVIRONMENT: Mountain
LOCATION: Steens Mountain Recreation Lands. From the town of Frenchglen, which lies approximately 61 miles south of Burns on State Highway 205, head east on Steens Mountain Road. In about 26 miles you'll see a road taking off to the left (east), with a sign pointing to the East Rim Viewpoint. Follow this to the end—about 0.4 mile—and begin walking north on a faint path that winds along the top of the rim.

This short rimtop ramble will bring you about as close as a person can get to realizing that old mountain notion of being able to look "all the way into tomorrow." (A shorter, but still expansive view—perhaps a look back at "roughly this morning"—can be had merely by turning around and facing west.) The east face of the tilted, 30-mile-long Steens Mountain Uplift nose-dives so sharply into the desert 5,000 feet below, that if you happen to have even the slightest case of acrophobia you may want to consider chaining yourself to your car before you venture anywhere close to the rim.

One of the first things you'll see at the foot of this mountain is a thin skin of sand, sagebrush, greasewood, hopsage, and shadscale cloaking the Alvord Desert. This is a hot, fabulously desolate place—the driest environment in the state of Oregon. And yet the small family groups of nomadic Indians who roamed here thousands of years ago fared better than you might imagine. While these people did eat jackrabbits, seeds, roots, rodents, lizards, and other desert offerings, they also had access to other, richer environments nearby. Bighorn sheep, elk, and deer could be hunted in the uplands, while salmon were plentiful in the Malheur River to the north. The wetlands of Malheur provided them with ducks, geese, and coots. The fact is that this region, as dry as parts of it may be, has more water and a greater variety of elevation-based ecosystems than any other in the Great Basin Desert.

As a group of pioneers headed for western Oregon in 1845 found out, the skill needed to prosper in desert environments is not

Bighorn Sheep

something to figure out as the need arises. While resting at Fort Boise after crossing the hot, dry reaches of southern Idaho's Snake River Plains, these weary emigrants found themselves collared by a man named Steve Meek (brother of Joe Meek, the famous trapper). Meek boasted that he knew a fine shortcut across the Oregon Desert that would shave 200 miles off the Oregon Trail; further, he would happily guide them over this route for the trifling sum of $5 per wagon.

Saving 200 miles meant saving about two weeks of travel. And to people who'd already been on the trail for four months, who were still clearing hundreds of miles of Idaho dust from their throats, the offer must have sounded like the answer to a prayer. After talking it over for a time, a large group of settlers decided to go for it. Unfortunately, Meek somehow lost his way near the Malheur River, and for six long weeks the party drifted in loose circles through the sand and sage. By the time they finally reached the Columbia River, 20 people were dead; another 20 were so badly off they died shortly thereafter.

As if that wasn't enough to ensure immortality for this ill-fated trip, a strange side story surfaced later. One of the members of the wagon train, a man named Dan Herron, supposedly picked up a couple pieces of shiny metal while looking for some cattle he'd lost near the head of the Malheur River. He took the stones back to show the others, who promptly judged them as worthless. (According to one version of this story, Dan later used them as fishing weights.) Four years later, at Sutter's Fort in California, a group of men who knew what they were talking about told poor Dan that he had in fact found gold. Several of the men joined Dan to search for the spot where he'd seen the nuggets, but it was never found again.

This tale is given a strange twist in the "blue bucket story"— a fabricated yarn first published in *The Oregonian*. Instead of Dan Herron finding the gold while out searching for cattle, in this story a 13-year-old girl spotted the nuggets while washing at a stream. Fascinated by the colors, she gathered up the biggest of the stones and took them back to the wagon train, accidentally leaving her blue bucket by the stream. Years later, when she gave the stones to her own kids to play with, her brother happened to see them and identified them as gold. Before long a number of people were out combing this remote area looking for that little blue bucket. Though completely untrue, this story, or similar versions of it, became so widespread that eventually the hapless wagon train was dubbed the "blue bucket train."

As you make your way above the steep, fluted ravines and rocky ledges of the eastern face, keep your eyes out for bighorn sheep below. Historically, these animals were plentiful in this area, but hunting and other human-related pressures caused them to vanish from the mountain by 1915. Eleven bighorn were taken from Hart Mountain National Wildlife Refuge in the early 1960s and placed along the eastern slope. Sixteen years later there were 150 animals plying these rugged cliffs and ravines, and today there are about 250 to 300.

A bighorn spinning dizzy pirouettes on the edge of oblivion is a performance you'll never forget. Except during their breeding season these animals spend most of their day in a cycle of eating and resting, the young sometimes scrambling after each other in a rockbound game of chase. No matter how relaxed a band of bighorn might appear, however, they are always in a state of alertness. Their incredible eyesight allows them to detect the slightest movement, and they'll dash for cover if they feel at all threatened.

Typically, just one ewe comes into estrus at a time, usually sometime during November or December. If she catches the attention of more than one ram, then the two males will square off in one of those skull-crunching duels that hurts to even think about. What we rarely see on television nature shows, though, is that rams don't just use their horns against each other; if a good chance comes to kick an opponent in the flanks, they'll take it. Six months later females give birth to a single lamb, delivered in the most out-of-the-way, inaccessible places imaginable.

Bighorn do not do well in stressful situations. Under conditions of overcrowding, for example, what would normally be a minor illness may quickly lead to death. For this reason, managing these magnificent animals in many parts of the West has been a tremendous challenge.

In just under a mile you'll reach our turnaround point, at a steeply cut ravine heading off to the southeast. (On the other side of the road is Little Blitzen Gorge—yet another example of the staggering power of glaciers.) At this point you may just want to take a seat and savor the scenery—a view that extends past the boundaries of Oregon, and well into the high deserts of northern Nevada and southern Idaho.

▪ IDAHO ▪

IDAHO

...

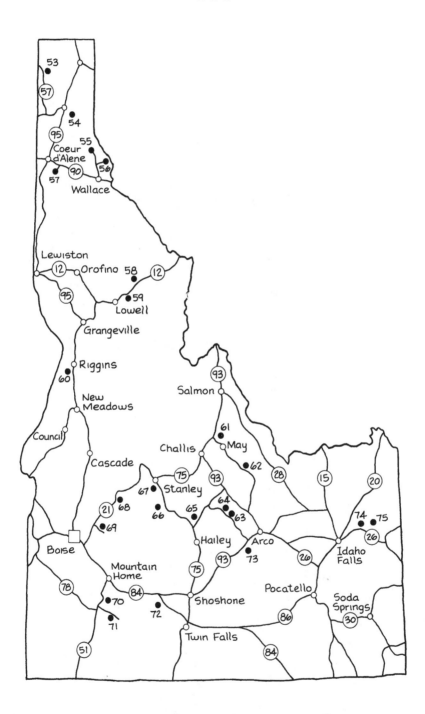

53
57
54
95
55
Coeur
d'Alene
90
56
57
Wallace

Lewiston
12
Orofino 58
12
95
59
Lowell
Grangeville

Riggins
60
New
Meadows
93
Salmon
Council
61
May
Cascade
Challis
62
75
93
28
15
20
Stanley
67
64
74
75
21
68
65
63
26
66
69
Hailey
Arco
Idaho
Boise
73
26
Falls
Mountain
Home
75
93
Pocatello
Soda
78
Springs
84
Shoshone
30
70
72
86
71
84
51
Twin Falls

Northern Idaho

WALK #53—NAVIGATION TRAIL

DISTANCE: 5.1 miles
ENVIRONMENT: Forest
LOCATION: Kaniksu National Forest (within the Idaho Panhandle national forests). From the town of Priest River, head north on State Road 57 for approximately 38 miles, to the village of Nordman. Turn right here (east) onto Forest Road 1339, and follow it for 12 miles to Beaver Creek Campground. Once inside the campground complex, follow the signs to the trailhead.

Nestled in the arms of the Selkirk Mountains, Upper Priest Lake is a vision from the past. Walking past these quiet groves of hemlock and cedar and river birch, a lone canoe paddle flashing on the waters of the lake, you can almost get a sense of what this country was like before waves of settlers began rolling through; before the British pushed into the lake country looking for furs; before the Jesuits and the Methodists began arm wrestling one another for control of Indian souls (Priest Lake take its name from this era); before the first of what would turn into $4 billion worth of precious metal was pulled from these mountains; before timber companies took over thousands of acres of old growth, often acquiring them for $1.25 to $2.50 an acre.

While the trek from Beaver Creek Campground to Upper Priest Lake is longer than many in this book, it's really a gentle woodland stroll, easily managed by a wide variety of age groups. (One note of caution: The trail crosses wet, muddy cedar and black cottonwood bottoms, so be sure you have appropriate footwear.) The first stretch of the path is through a fine middle-aged forest, stitched around the edges with beargrass, pipsissewa, yellow

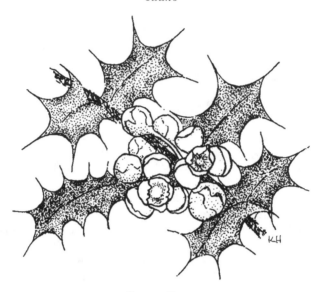

Oregon Grape

violets, trillium, and bunchberry, as well as the hollylike evergreen leaves of Oregon grape. Oregon grape, among the most important of all medicinal plants, is one that you'll come across time and time again during your forays into the woods of the Northwest. Certain alkaloids in the roots of Oregon grape give the plant a number of unique medicinal qualities. The presence of *berberis*, for example, a muscle stimulant, made its use popular during childbirth to ease the passage of the placenta. (Berberis is also what produces the beautiful yellow dye extracted from Oregon grape.) Indians and settlers alike used Oregon grape as a diuretic and antiseptic, while a tea from the roots was for years a standard treatment for venereal disease.

At about 2.3 miles into the walk is a small cabin, off to the left of the trail. This was built between 1910 and 1920 by a man named Alva Allen, who lived in Spokane and worked for the railroad. Alva and his wife Myrtle christened this humble little abode the "Allen A Dale," and spent many fine times here wrapped in the thick weave of wilderness that ran from their door. Curiously, in a diary the Allens kept, now on file in the archives at Washington State University, they mention the wonderful view the cabin afforded of Upper Priest Lake. This view was actually thanks to an enormous fire that burned the entire west side of the lake sometime in the 1880s; as you can see, the Allens' view has since been shut off by a curtain of timber.

In another 0.2 mile you'll find your own views of Upper Priest Lake. Shortly afterward—about 100 yards past a bridged stream crossing—is a very faint trail taking off to the right. This short path leads into Plowboy Campground, a dispersed camping area situated on a nice slice of shoreline. From here you'll be able to glean spectacular views of the lake basin, framed to the east and north by the dramatic green and gray folds of the Selkirk Mountains. Though they've been used and abused in years past, the Selkirks are still a magnificent mountain range—a mix of glacial valleys, abrupt ridgelines, and thick, wet forests of cedar, hemlock, and Douglas fir. (About 10 miles to the east and slightly north of Plowboy Campground is Long Canyon, where you can still find wonderful groves of 500-year-old western redcedar.)

The Selkirks are also home to the only known group of woodland caribou in the United States; it is a small herd, making regular runs in and out of British Columbia. This member of the deer family spends January through May on the high, sparsely forested ridges of the Selkirks, where the snow is compacted enough to allow easy travel. Snow walking is also made easier because caribou have such large feet, their hooves spreading some 6 inches across. In the high country they subsist primarily on arboreal lichen—that greenish-gray, mosslike plant that you may have seen hanging from the branches of conifers. The catch is that arboreal lichen tends to grow only on trees that are at least a century old. Intense clear-cutting has sharply reduced these important feeding grounds; in addition, roads constructed during logging operations have resulted in greater access to the herd by hunters, who frequently mistake them for deer or elk. Concern about inbreeding has led to an effort to increase the Selkirk herd, primarily by augmenting it with transplants from British Columbia. It's a heroic attempt to restore an animal that, at least in this region, has long been skating on the brink of extinction.

WALK #54—MINERAL POINT

DISTANCE:	0.9 mile
ENVIRONMENT:	Mountain
LOCATION:	Kaniksu National Forest (within the Idaho Panhandle national forests). From the town of Sandpoint, head south on U.S. Highway 95 for approximately 6 miles. Go 0.2 mile past mile marker 469, and turn left (east) onto Sagle Road. Follow this for approximately 7.3 miles, at which point you'll reach a small road taking off to the right, with a sign that says "Mineral Point—6 miles." Take this right fork and proceed for 1.5 miles, turning left at Garfield Bay on a village street going uphill. Three-tenths mile from this last junction, take a right. Our trailhead is 3.6 miles down this road; when you come to a fork, follow the Forest Service signs for trail 82.

This lovely interpretive trail was constructed in 1989 to honor Brent "Jake" Jacobson—a 41-year-old Forest Service law enforcement officer who was gunned down while pursuing two fugitives in northern Idaho during the winter of 1989. Jake was the first Forest Service law enforcement officer ever killed in the line of duty. It would be hard to imagine a finer tribute than this 0.9-mile nature path, hung on a lush, forested hillside high above the shining waters of Lake Pend Oreille. An interpretive brochure, produced by the Sandpoint Ranger District, corresponds to numbered posts along the trail; be sure to pick one up before you begin your walk.

One of the striking features of the Idaho Panhandle forests is their incredible lushness. This path begins in a beautiful tapestry of Douglas fir, maple, and ponderosa pine, then carries you in 0.4 mile to a bottomland thick with moisture-loving western redcedar and Pacific yew. Along the way the path is lined with mats of twisted stalk, Oregon grape, columbine, fireweed, violet, lupine, false Solomon's seal, fringe cup, trillium, strawberry, and calypso orchid.

You'll have gone less than 0.1 mile before coming to the first good view of Lake Pend Oreille—a perch that in spring comes

Columbine

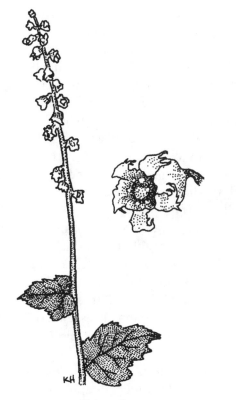

Fringe Cups

wrapped in cream-colored serviceberry blossoms, as well as the warm yellow heads of arrowleaf balsamroot. Lake Pend Oreille is in places more than 1,000 feet deep, excavated by great tongues of glacial ice that flowed south out of Canada more than 100,000 years ago. (Major ice flows were pouring out of Canada as recently as 12,000 years ago; most geologists, however, believe that these more recent glaciers wouldn't have been substantial enough to excavate a 1,000-foot-deep basin this far south.)

While the actual excavation of the Lake Pend Oreille Basin is nothing to sneeze at, it pales in comparison to another icy phenomenon that occurred on this site—one of the most spectacular geological events in the world. The great lobes of ice that flowed down from Canada eventually formed a mammoth ice dam along the eastern edge of Lake Pend Oreille, cutting off the flow of water from the Clark Fork River. Foot by foot the Clark Fork drainage began to fill, forming a lake (known as Glacial Lake Missoula) that reached a depth of over 4,000 feet. And then an astounding thing happened. The block of ice forming the dam began to float and then break into pieces, causing a sudden release of 500 cubic miles of water, thundering across the land at speeds of 45 miles per hour. Some researchers speculate that at maximum flow, the release was 10 times the volume of water present in all the world's rivers combined! This raging wall of water scoured out deep ravines throughout eastern Washington, filled the Columbia River Gorge with 1,000 feet of churning water, and caused enormous floods as far west as Oregon's Willamette Valley. This process of ice damming, filling, and then flooding happened not once, but dozens of times, though the force and power of that first great release was never equaled.

From this vista point the trail continues to descend through the forest, soon reaching another splendid lookout—the memorial site for Brent Jacobson. The path descends quickly from here, reaching the cedar bottoms at just over 0.3 mile. At this point you'll come to a fork in the trail; turn left, and proceed past a shaded garden of trillium, bedstraw, and pipsissewa. Indian peoples of the Northwest used solutions made from pipsissewa for a variety of ailments, including a tea to relieve fever and a wash for sore eyes. Many of the settlers who adopted the plant relied on it as a treatment for kidney disorders, an application that science has verified to some degree. Pipsissewa is found not only in moist coniferous forests across North America, but in Asia and Europe as well.

From here the trail makes a small loop through groves of ponderosa, Douglas fir, western redcedar, and yew. This is a quiet, sheltered world, rich in the kind of magic still woven across so much of the Idaho Panhandle.

Pipsissewa

WALK #55—INDEPENDENCE CREEK
NATIONAL RECREATION TRAIL

DISTANCE: 3.6 miles

ENVIRONMENT: Mountain

LOCATION: Coeur d'Alene National Forest (within the Idaho Panhandle national forests). From Interstate 90 west of Pinehurst, take exit 43 and head north on Forest Road 9, a road that follows along the south bank of the Coeur d'Alene River. In about 23.5 miles you'll see Road 9 heading off to the east; you continue north along the Coeur d'Alene River on Forest Road 208. Continue on Road 208 for approximately 30 miles, at which point you'll make a right turn onto Forest Road 3099. (Don't panic if at about 4 miles before this junction, Road 208 suddenly changes its number, becoming Forest Road 6310.) Follow Road 3099 for 0.3 mile, and then turn left onto Forest Road 825, a narrow two-track road that heads down a slight hill. Our trailhead is about 0.9 mile from this last junction. (Those with large vehicles could park at the intersection of roads 3099 and 6310; this would add 2.4 miles to the round-trip walk.)

Those who intend to take this warm, sun-drenched stroll up Independence Creek should first arm themselves with a Coeur d'Alene National Forest map. The fact is that there are many ways of getting into this area—from the wild shores of Lake Pend Oreille or the banks of the Clark Fork; from the flanks of Honey Mountain or the North Fork of the Coeur d'Alene River. No matter how you come, though, getting here will involve considerable, though thoroughly enjoyable, driving.

The route you'll be walking follows an old wagon road. Built around 1910, this road connected Lake Pend Oreille and nearby mining camps with Independence and Tepee Creek valleys. Over the 20 years that followed, the route was regularly traveled by homesteaders, loggers, Forest Service rangers, and firefighters.

White-tailed Deer

Most of the improvements that were made along Independence Creek during this period, from cabins and corrals to a splash dam used to raise the water level for floating logs, have long since disappeared. Today there remains only a wonderful weave of clear water, rounded mountains cloaked in conifers, and meadows spiked with thick mats of grass and wildflowers. If there's any walk in this book where you'll ignore the suggested turnaround point and just keep going, this will likely be it.

The walk begins with a 0.5-mile climb through a pleasant forest of Douglas fir, white pine, and an occasional cluster of aspen. This is also a good place to spot huckleberry, Oregon grape, violets, pipsissewa, as well as large swaths of a shrub by the name of false box (also known as box myrtlewood, or myrtle box leaf). False box—commonly found in Douglas fir, aspen, and lodgepole forests—typically grows 1 to 3 feet high and sports opposite-toothed evergreen leaves and tiny clusters of raspberry-colored flowers. Both white-tailed and mule deer are big fans of false box, especially in winter, when other foods can be tough to find.

Another evergreen shrub you'll see among the more moist sections of this walk is snowbrush—a shiny green plant with three distinct veins running up from the base of each toothed leaf. Like false box, snowbrush is heavily browsed by deer in the winter months; if you look closely, you'll see broken stems where the animals have been eating. An interesting quality of this, and many other species of *Ceanothus*, is that the flowers contain a glycoside called "saponin," which has properties similar to soap. Indeed, early Indian peoples, and later settlers, used snowbrush blooms extensively as a soap substitute.

As you begin to descend the small divide you gained at 0.5 mile, the character of the landscape undergoes a splendid transition. Sweeping views open up of the wild mountains to the west, out of which Independence Creek comes pouring like a river of jewels. After you cross a fine little stream at 0.8 mile framed by willow and false hellebore, the path rounds an open, south-facing slope. The added warmth afforded by southern exposure causes this hill to bloom earlier than other sections of the trail. And it does so in no uncertain terms, with scattered gardens of Oregon grape, lungwort, blue-eyed Mary, phlox, blue violets, and larkspur.

At just over 1 mile the trail drops off this sunny slope into a young conifer forest sprinkled with trillium, goldthread, and coarse tufts of beargrass. Every five to seven years beargrass puts forth a towering 3-foot-tall stalk, atop of which rests a raceme of beautiful white flowers. The leaves of this plant are extremely tough, and are virtually ignored as a food source by almost all big game species except the hearty Rocky Mountain goat. Indians throughout the Northwest dried and bleached the tough, shiny basal leaves of beargrass and then wove them into baskets.

In another 0.2 mile the path joins the grassy north bank of Independence Creek. From here the stream will be an almost constant companion, offering you literally dozens of cool, quiet places to rest or picnic. At 1.6 miles you'll cross Mirror Creek and pass by Emmerson Ridge Trail taking off to the right, and in another 0.2 mile, reach our turnaround on the wild green shores of Emmerson Creek. If you'd like to grab an even bigger scoop of solitude, make your way up through the cool shade of Emmerson Creek for a hundred yards or so, where there will be no one to bother you but an occasional dipper, white-tailed deer, mountain chickadee, ruby-crowned kinglet, and, if your luck is very good, the regal, reclusive lynx. This latter animal is perhaps as little known as any mammal in America. It's frequently confused with the

Lynx

bobcat, but bobcats are found living not in thick woods like this one, but more in open patchworks of shrubs and along forest edges. Lynx have a range of 6 to 8 square miles, and subsist on a diet of squirrels, mice, birds, and, whenever possible, snowshoe hares. In fact, in some regions snowshoe hares are such an important part of this animal's diet that the death rate of young lynx kittens exactly mirrors reductions in the population of hares.

WALK #56—SETTLERS GROVE OF ANCIENT CEDARS

DISTANCE: 2 miles
ENVIRONMENT: Forest
LOCATION: Coeur d'Alene National Forest (within the Idaho Panhandle national forests). From the town of Wallace, head north on 6th Street, toward Dobson Pass. Follow this road for approximately 16.5 miles, and turn right, just after crossing the Coeur d'Alene River. Make another right in 1.7 miles, onto Forest Road 9, and take this eastward for just under 3 miles, where you'll turn left onto Forest Road 152. About 1.3 miles after this last turn the road will fork; stay to the left, turning onto Forest Road 805. Settlers Grove of Ancient Cedars is about 6 miles down Road 805.

No one finds themselves at The Settlers Grove of Ancient Cedars by accident, stumbling across it as they fly down the exit ramp looking for a rest room. Reaching this place requires traversing long twists of narrow roads. The good news is that the trip itself is in some ways as fine as the destination. There are a couple of tantalizing views of the beautiful Coeur d'Alene River along the way, as well as a lovely drive along the bottom of Pritchard Creek. The last 6 miles of forest road have more picnic sites and camping spots than you could shake a cedar at, most fronted by the delightful West Fork of Eagle Creek.

The trail itself will pull you in gently, offering a lazy meander back and forth over Eagle Creek. Slowly but surely, moderate-sized cedar and Douglas fir give way to bigger and bigger trees, until by about 0.25 mile into the walk you're in a land of utter giants. Try to imagine what it would be like if this grove of creek-bottom cedars were not an anomaly but a normal, everyday swath of forest—if such woods could still be found cloaking river and stream bottoms across much of the Northwest. Admittedly, some would characterize such daydreaming as a rather shameless longing for the past. But the fact is that when you're steeped in the shade of trees that are this big, some of which were already a century old when Joan of Arc was raising the siege of Orleans, such fantasies arise almost as a matter of course.

At about 0.5 mile, just downstream from the fourth crossing of the West Fork of Eagle Creek, you'll see a large downed log—one of several lining this trail. The small hemlocks, Douglas fir, and patches of moss growing out of the top of this fallen giant are good examples of why such downed trees are often referred to as "nurse logs." Bacteria present in the wood of the dead log take nitrogen from the air and convert it to a form that can be used by new plants—a process referred to as *nitrogen fixation*. What's more, trees

Red-breasted Nuthatch

that actually fall into streams, like the jumble of toppled conifers you saw near the second bridge crossing, may be responsible for most of the organic nutrients found in the stream system, the reason being that they hold back debris long enough for it to be biologically broken down.

And that's only the beginning of how valuable these fallen giants can be. The limbs and root tangles serve as perches, feeding sites, or nesting areas for winter wrens, thrushes, juncos, woodpeckers, western flycatchers, chestnut-backed chickadees, and red-breasted nuthatches. Blue grouse dance for mates on the tops of fallen trees, while squirrels use them as feeding tables from which they can keep a close eye on the surrounding terrain. The truth is that there are literally dozens and dozens of birds, mammals, and invertebrates that use such downed timber every day. Such trees are hardly "wasted," as some people would have you believe, simply because they never make it to the lumber mill.

At 0.7 mile is yet another stream crossing, this one marked by a lovely downstream vista of timbered islands and braided channels. On either side of the bridge keep your eyes open for violets, trillium, ginger, and western goldthread. Our turn-around is completely arbitrary. From a short distance past this last bridge a faint trail continues to climb along the West Fork of Eagle Creek, topping out in just under 4 miles at an old forest road that heads north to Bloom Peak—a 5,800-foot promontory sitting smack dab on the forested ridge that divides Idaho and Montana.

WALK #57—MINERAL RIDGE
NATIONAL RECREATION TRAIL

DISTANCE: 2.7 miles
ENVIRONMENT: Mountain
LOCATION: Bureau of Land Management. From Interstate 90 east of Coeur d'Alene, head south on State Road 97 for 2.3 miles. At this point you'll see the Mineral Ridge picnic area and trailhead off to your left. (If you cross the bridge over Beauty Creek, you've gone too far.)

While on any given weekend the Mineral Ridge Trail can seem rather thick with people, those who rouse themselves for an early morning trek will end up wrapped in plenty of solitude. This is also the time of day when you'll hear a particularly fine chorus of birdsong, the performance courtesy of local nuthatches, chickadees, wrens, jays, and thrushes. Although the Mineral Ridge Trail makes a steady climb of 735 feet over about 1.5 miles, there's no shortage of engaging diversions and rest stops along the way—pungent coniferous forests, clusters of wildflowers and blooming shrubs, and beautiful views of Lake Coeur d'Alene. This was the first recreation site in Idaho to be developed by the Bureau of Land Management. Started in the winter of 1963, it's a showcase of what this agency can do for recreation when they put their minds and pocketbooks to the task. (The BLM has produced a trail guide for this walk that corresponds with numbered posts along the path; be sure to pick one up at the trailhead information sign.)

The trail rises through a nice mix of ponderosa pine and Douglas fir, spiked here and there with a few hemlocks, white pines, and tamaracks. If you can make it here during blooming season, you'll also be treated to the showy blossoms of pea vine, strawberry, Oregon grape, long-flowered lungwort, white clover, fairy slipper, and waterleaf. This latter plant, which is also known as ballhead waterleaf, produces its ball-shaped cluster of violet flowers early in the spring, before the soil on Mineral Ridge has had a chance to dry out. The young leaves of waterleaf are very succulent, and were popular as a cooked green with settlers and Indian peoples alike.

At about 0.8 mile you'll reach marker post 11 at Radio Viewpoint, perched above a hill sprinkled with arrowleaf balsamroot. As the BLM trail guide explains, this area and many other areas along Mineral Ridge were mined extensively during the first few decades of the 20th century—particularly during World War I, when metal prices were high. As you walk this path you'll occasionally see shallow depressions on either side of the trail. These are the remains of Mineral Ridge mining activity.

When we think of mining, it's often a romantic image of a lone prospector kneeling beside some icy stream, cradling a gold pan in his weathered hands. The Idaho Panhandle did have its share of loners as late as the early 1880s, some of whom were farmers from the Palouse country to the west, who worked their claims around the planting and harvesting of crops. But the "easy pickings" disappeared quickly. What's more, it was silver, not gold, that formed the lion's share of wealth in the Coeur d'Alene mining district; and silver had to be mined through expensive tunneling operations, and then refined. This meant that by the late 1800s, mining here was strictly big business—a game wherein powerful corporations from the East called the tunes to which miners would dance. If something happened in the industry to tarnish profits, then it was the miners who were expected to take it on the chin. When silver prices started to fall at the same time that railroad freight charges were rising in the 1890s, for example, mine owners responded by making sharp cutbacks in miners' wages. When workers banded together and struck as a protest, they were fired and replaced by nonunion members, most of whom worked under the protection of armed guards.

The tension between management and labor grew worse and worse in the Coeur d'Alene until, in the summer of 1892, angry debate was replaced by gunfire and dynamite. Just as it seemed that the miners might win the battle, having rounded up the scabs and ousted them from the district, Governor Norman Willey decided to end the war altogether by declaring martial law. State and federal troops descended on the district en masse, imprisoning more than 300 people in bull pens—not just miners, mind you, but virtually anyone who corporate spies had identified as sympathetic to the miners' plight. Most ended up staying in these hot, stinking prisons for over seven weeks, waiting for a hearing. Eventually, 25 union leaders were sent to Boise to stand trial, many of whom later did time in prison. Federal troops were sent in once again seven years later after union members dynamited the Bunker Hill and Sullivan mine complex; that incident led to nearly 700 men being sent to the bull pens.

The Coeur d'Alene became the biggest mining district in the entire state of Idaho, and one of the most lucrative of the western United States. More than a third of all silver produced in this country comes from this district; to date, over a billion ounces have been plucked from the nooks and crannies of these rolling mountains.

Continue climbing for another 0.5 mile to the 2,875-foot summit of Mineral Ridge, and turn left. A short distance after gaining the ridge you'll reach Caribou Cabin; built in 1963, it offers fine views of Wolf Lodge Bay to the north. If you happen to be here in early spring, scan the steep hillsides below the Caribou Cabin for the beautiful nodding yellow blooms of glacier lilies. While the bulbs of this plant can be eaten raw or cooked, they are so difficult to unearth that few Indian tribes ever made them a mainstay of their spring diet.

From here the path makes a pleasant traverse of a high, forested ridge, the quilt of conifers broken here and there by serviceberry, wild rose, ocean spray, and ninebark. At marker post 22, just before the trail begins a sharp descent back to the parking area, you'll find a bench offering a spectacular view of Lake Coeur d'Alene. While you might assume that this lake is the product of glaciation, like some of those to the north, that's true only indirectly. When what we consider to be the first great ice age poured out of Canada about 100,000 years ago, the mammoth sheets of ice actually stopped before they got this far. In their wake, however, was a moraine of till and outwash debris that ultimately dammed the St. Joe River. Consequently, the St. Joe Valley filled with water, creating the magnificent lake you see before you today.

Central Idaho

WALK #58—LOCHSA RIVER HISTORIC TRAIL

DISTANCE:	2.5 miles
ENVIRONMENT:	Mountain
LOCATION:	Clearwater National Forest. From U.S. Highway 112, turn north on Fish Creek Road, located at about mile marker 120. Shortly after making this turn you'll see the trail crossing a wooden bridge on your left; continue down the road until you've found a suitable parking place.

September 16, 1805
I have been wet and as cold in every part as I ever was in my life, indeed I was at one time fearful my feet would freeze in the thin moccasins which I wore.

—*William Clark*
writing from the Lolo Trail
about 25 miles from this trailhead

September 17, 1805
The snow melted so that the water stood in the trail over our moccasins in some places. Very slippery, and bad traveling for our horses. We ascend very high and rocky mountains; some bald places on the top of the mountains, high rocks standing up and high precipices.

—*Joseph Whitehouse*
member of the Lewis and Clark expedition

September 18, 1805
This morning we finished the last of our colt. We supped on a scant portion of portable soup, a little bear's oil, and about 20 pounds of candles form our stock of provisions, our only resources being our guns and horses. This is but a poor dependence where there is nothing upon earth but ourselves, a few pheasants, small grey squirrels, and a blue bird of the vulture kind about the size of a turtle dove or jay bird. Used snow for cooking.

—*Meriwether Lewis*
(The "blue bird," incidentally, was a Steller's jay.)

The following day, September 19, the Lewis and Clark party reached Sherman Peak, a promontory lying just 6 miles north of where you now stand, along the famous Lolo Trail. To their utter delight, this time they gazed out not on another line of mountains, but on a vast prairie—home of the long-awaited Columbia River. Party member Patrick Glass tells of the feeling running through the men on that autumn morning: "When this discovery was made there was as much joy and rejoicing among the corps as happens among passengers at sea who have experienced a dangerous protracted voyage, when they first discover land on the long looked for coast."

As much as any other route of the region, the Lolo Trail gained an infamous reputation among explorers and trappers. There were several reasons for this, as former Regional Forester Ralph Space points out in his fine book, *The Clearwater Story*. First of all, timber grows thick in these mountains, which means that riding unmaintained trails is like poking your way through a pile of pickup sticks. Also, a number of major saddles cut the route, requiring that travelers make a series of steep climbs and falls, sometimes losing and gaining 1,000 feet. General O. O. Howard, a pious Army man often referred to as the "praying general," had this to say about the Lolo Trail: "Conceive this climbing ridge after ridge, in the wildest wilderness, with the only possible pathway filled with timber, small and large, crossed and criss-crossed; and now, while the horses and mules are feeding on unnutritious wire grass, you will not wonder at only sixteen miles a day."

Our walk in this lower country, south of the Lolo Trail, traverses a cool forest, finally coming out on a series of flower-bedecked slopes; from those hillsides you'll have wonderful views of the Lochsa River to the southwest, and the high, rugged ridges of the Selway–Bitterroot Wilderness to the south. The first 0.6 mile of pathway requires a steady climb, though the grade is certainly manageable. Helping to ease the pain is a delightful array of common plants, including Douglas fir, white pine, and mountain hemlock. This is also a good stretch to see ocean spray, queen's cup, twisted stalk, twinflower, serviceberry, thimbleberry, path-finder, strawberry, bedstraw, bunchberry, and both sword and maidenhair ferns. Pathfinder, incidentally, is a 1- to 2-foot-high plant with large, arrow-shaped leaves, green on top and silver underneath. It was this coloration that led to the plant's common

Sword Fern

name of pathfinder; it's easy to follow the path of someone who steps through a patch of these plants, as the silver side of the turned leaves shows up easily from yards away.

This entire area was burned during a fire in 1934. A heroic effort by a crew of about 200 Civilian Conservation Corps men kept the Lochsa Ranger Station—just east of where you turned off the highway for this walk—from burning to the ground. Indeed, by the morning of August 18 nearly everything but the station was reduced to ashes. At one point a large spark landed on a fire hose, causing it to burst; it was only the frenzied efforts of men carrying bucket after bucket of water and operating hand pumps until they dropped from exhaustion that saved the Lochsa station.

Built in the mid-1920s, this trail was used for nearly 40 years by the Forest Service to supply both fire lookouts and the Lochsa Ranger Station. It was given new life in 1990, and now runs along the length of the Lochsa River from Split Creek Trailhead (mile marker 111) to Sherman Creek (mile marker 123). Further, the route is a part of the Idaho Centennial North-South Trail, which runs the entire length of the state.

Along the early section of the path are several small open areas, offering tantalizing views of the Lochsa River and the Selway–Bitterroot country to the south. The real glory spot, however, is at about 1.1 miles. Here the forest melts away into meadows strewn with wildflowers—scarlet gilia, yarrow, St. Johnswort, stonecrop, Clarkia, paintbrush, and penstemon, to name but a few.

Add to this a magnificent view stretching up and down the silvery twists of the Lochsa River, the mountains on either side wrapped in thick blankets of timber, and a bright blue ribbon of summer sky stretching overhead.

Note that by continuing around the next lobe of mountain you'll reach Otter Slide Creek—a beautiful stream and an excellent place to lunch on a warm summer day.

WALK #59—MAJOR FENN NATURE TRAIL

DISTANCE: 1 mile
ENVIRONMENT: Forest
LOCATION: Clearwater National Forest. From U.S. Highway 12 along the Lochsa River, turn into the Major Fenn Picnic Area, which is located 0.2 mile west of mile marker 108. To reach the nature trail, cross a small bridge over a flood channel, and turn left. Numbered posts correspond to a plant identification guide, copies of which you should find near the parking area.

When you discover that the Major Fenn area contains a large "coastal disjunct plant population," your first instinct may be to run off and phone the exterminator. What this botany-speak means is that along this short trail you'll pass fully 15 plants that aren't really supposed to be here at all, but belong 400 miles to the west, on the coasts of Oregon and Washington. You'll also find identified many wild plants common to much of northern Idaho; in fact, walking this trail offers a perfect preview of what you'll see on other hikes in the region. The Clearwater National Forest and the Clearwater Valley Garden Club have done a splendid job on a plant identification guide, located at the trailhead, keyed to 15 stops along the route. Perhaps the only fly in the ointment is that the trail lies rather close to the highway, though much of the traffic noise can be avoided by planning an early morning visit.

Since the Garden Club has made certain you'll get your fill of plant information, let's talk a bit about the cultural history of this area.

Of first concern is Major Fenn, whose name graces not only this trail and picnic area, but also a mountain peak in the Selway Crags. Major Fenn's parents were among the first to settle in central Idaho during the 1860s. They had a son named Frank who, along with six other children, attended Idaho's first public school in a town along the Salmon River by the name of Florence—a town, incidentally, which by the summer of 1862 was producing $50,000 worth of gold a day! Frank left the boomtown life for the adventure of the military, graduating from the Naval Academy and carving out a distinguished record in the Spanish-American War. He eventually returned to Idaho, and wore the hat of everything from lawyer, to teacher, to newspaper publisher. Fenn eventually landed a position as the first supervisor of the Clearwater National Forest.

Of course there were others living in these rugged mountains long before such settlers started writing their histories across the land. Archaeological finds indicate that people were roaming this region 12,000 years ago—gathering seeds and berries, taking fish and mussels from the rivers, and hunting the great woolly mammoth with spears. As the centuries passed they became more and more proficient at gathering food, especially the salmon, which they caught using special fishing platforms built over the Lochsa, Clearwater, and Selway rivers.

With the introduction of the horse during the 1700s, a drastic change came about for the people we know historically as the Nez Perce. Not only did the Nez Perce use the horse to expand their hunting grounds to the buffalo country of Montana (often traveling the Lolo Trail, which lies just to the north, they also proved to be exceptional breeders—perhaps most notably with regard to the beautiful Appaloosa.

The political system of the Nez Perce was based on a loose network of autonomous family bands that the elders advised, but did not command. This system, which greatly honored the sanctity of the individual and his immediate family, made attempts by the U.S. government to push blanket treaties utterly ridiculous. Even if certain elders did sign such agreements with the American government—and some of them did—it meant nothing to those who weren't interested. When treaty makers tried to talk Chief Joseph into selling Nez Perce lands, he told them rather matter-of-factly that such a request was out the question, that "the earth is too sacred to be valued by or sold for silver and gold."

River Otter

All in all, the number of tales running up and down the Lochsa would fill volumes. (*Lochsa*, incidentally, is a Flathead Indian word meaning "rough water.) An old rifle found in the hills might be that of a lone hunter killed in a bad fall on the Lolo Trail; an ax-hewn log high on a river bank might be from a raft used by hunters trying to escape the cold slap of winter; an overgrown, unmarked grave might be that of dance hall girl Moose Creek Molly; and the patch of ground you camp on some cold fall night might be the same one used by Lewis and Clark on their epic journey to the Pacific Ocean in 1805. Much as in any other forest in Idaho, here in the Clearwater the old days seem still wonderfully fresh and alive.

Besides looking for the plants described in the Major Fenn Plant Identification Brochure, would-be botanists might also want to keep an eye out for heal-all, yarrow, mullein, twinflower, twisted stalk, queen's cup, and, on the final stretch of trail along the flood channel, tall weaves of orchard grass and the white blooms of dogwood. Should you fail to find one of the trail brochures waiting for you, following is a list of each plant and the post that marks it.

1) sword fern
2) serviceberry
3) Pacific yew
4) Douglas hawthorne
5) kinnikinnick
6) beargrass
7) Oregon grape
8) black cottonwood
9) red-osier dogwood
10) snowberry
11) horsetail
12) ocean spray
13) syringa
14) paper birch
15) cascara

WALK #60—RAPID RIVER CANYON

DISTANCE: 2 miles
ENVIRONMENT: Desert
LOCATION: Nez Perce National Forest. From the town of Riggins, head south on U.S. Highway 95 for about 4 miles. Turn right onto Forest Road 2114, following the signs for the Rapid River Fish Hatchery. Our trail takes off from the fish hatchery, up a rutted dirt road climbing to the southwest. *Note:* Please be sure not to block any gates or hatchery thoroughfares.

Walking through the bottom of this canyon, as often as not you'll be rubbing elbows with a lush weave of life—one you might not have believed possible from looking at the dry, grassy hills visible from U.S. Highway 95. Appropriately, Rapid River has been classified as a National Wild and Scenic River, which means that its singular beauty will be here to enjoy for a long time to come.

Park your car near the fish hatchery, and walk up the steep two-track that climbs to the southwest. In 50 yards or so the road ends and the trail begins, clinging to a bench high above the roar of the river. The plants you'll see along any given stretch of this walk will, of course, depend to some extent on what time of year you visit. Spring and early summer visitors will find themselves shuffling through a pleasant mat of salsify, fillaree, rice grass, bluegrass, and balsamroot. Notice how the north slope, on the other side of Rapid River, is cloaked with much thicker robes—ponderosa, maple, and various deciduous shrubs—than the south side, which is more thoroughly rung dry by the rays of the sun. Each time you round one of these hills, watch how the vegetation changes. Serviceberry will show up in one ravine, its lovely cream-colored blossoms flying from the ends of its branches, while on dry, rocky outcrops you'll find little but greasewood—a plant thoroughly accustomed to living in the desert.

Long ago, the edge of the continent was at roughly the place where the Salmon River is today. Lying offshore of this ancient coast were a series of volcanic and sedimentary "island arcs," which eventually collided against the edge of the westward-moving continent. The metamorphosed sedimentary rock you'll be passing on this walk was actually a part of just such an island arc. To add even more color (or confusion), Rapid River traces almost exactly a major *thrust fault*, which is a horizontal line where one sliver of the earth's crust was thrust over another. Indeed, the very location of Rapid River may have been controlled by this fault.

Much later, this entire portion of Idaho, rather flat at the time, experienced a major uplift. Rivers and streams that once flowed rather gently began moving faster and faster, cutting through the rock like a knife pulled through a tub of butter—creating extraordinary gorges like Rapid River, as well as the Salmon River Canyon to the northeast and Hells Canyon to the west. The rather lilting, rolling terrain you see at the tops of these canyons is the remnant of this old erosional surface.

Wallflower

At 0.5 mile you'll come upon the first of a long line of small, twisted trees known as curl-leaf mountain mahogany. This tree, which may live for 300 years, gets the first part of its name from the fact that the smooth edges of the thick, leathery leaves curl under slightly. As for the "mountain mahogany" part, the only resemblance to the mahogany of the tropics is that both woods are dark and heavy—so heavy, in fact, that they won't float. Curl-leaf mountain mahogany is found growing in some of the driest, harshest conditions in the West, from the sandstone canyons of Arizona to the dry eastern flanks of the Sierra Nevada; from the blistering Mojave to the high deserts east of the Cascades. Members of this genus have developed a rather ingenious means of dealing with their harsh surroundings. Seeds are born on long, straight, rather feathery-looking plumes. Once these plumes fall from the tree and begin to dry, they twist like a corkscrew—a phenomenon that can actually drill the seed into the ground.

Soon the trail leaves this rather dry landscape, with its sporadic clusters of paintbrush, arrowleaf balsamroot, and wallflower, to join the thick vegetation along the river. By 0.75 mile you'll be side by side with ocean spray, hawthorn, ninebark, and serviceberry.

A mile into the walk you'll see a "1" painted on a rock outcropping. Continue just past this point, climbing to a small promontory that affords splendid views both up and down Rapid River. This blend of dry, soft-shouldered hills sliced by a cool twist of water is pure Idaho. To me it's one of the more lighthearted landscapes—a bright, spartan collage bringing together the best of desert, mountain, and prairie.

WALK #61—MORSE CREEK

DISTANCE: 3.6 miles
ENVIRONMENT: Forest
LOCATION: Challis National Forest. From U.S. Highway 93 at the tiny town of Ellis, turn southeast along the north side of the Pahsimeroi River, following a road that leads through the village of May. Follow this for 10.7 miles to Forest Road 094 (a small landing strip is at the southeast corner of this intersection). Follow Road 094 east for just under 7 miles to the Morse Creek Campground. Our walk—trail 72—takes off on a narrow road to the left just before you cross a bridge leading into the campground. *Note:* Much of Road 094 is narrow and one lane, not suitable for large vehicles or those pulling trailers.

Welcome to some of the most classic sage-covered basin and range country to be found anywhere in the Northwest. The lonely Pahsimeroi Valley runs for miles between the timbered flanks of the Lemhi and Lost River ranges, easily overwhelming those not accustomed to such incredible sprawls of open country. Most visitors to Idaho never end up anywhere close to this area, opting instead for the Pioneer or Sawtooth Mountains, or the big lakes and thick green forests of the Panhandle. Yet those willing to expend the energy needed to reach these more remote regions of the southeast will find no shortage of reward.

Before you leave the Pahsimeroi Valley for the cool timber of the Lemhi Range, look carefully across the sage flats for pronghorn, which are as plentiful here as anywhere in the state. If ever there was an animal built for this dry, wide-open country, the pronghorn is it. Looking at the faces of these animals through field glasses, notice how the eyes stick out from the side of the skull, offering an astonishing degree of peripheral vision. Add to that the fact that pronghorn can see small movements miles away—some suggest their sight is equivalent to 8-power binoculars—and you begin to understand that no one sneaks up on these guys.

Pronghorn

Pronghorn have been clocked over short distances at nearly 70 miles per hour, which makes them the fastest animal on the continent (remarkably, the young can outrun a human when just four days old!). Also, these animals can subsist on the scantiest of range vegetation, and can also go without water for extremely long periods of time.

Our walk begins on the north side of Morse Creek, along a broad green line of aspen, alder, and cottonwood; there's also thimbleberry, red-osier dogwood, and wild rose. Besides being beautiful to look at, roses have had a long history of use throughout the world. Native peoples of this region considered the wild rose to have significant medicinal value, and used it to treat everything from nose bleeds to sore eyes to diarrhea. When Great Britain was unable to import citrus during World War II, tons of rose fruits, or "hips" were collected to make a vitamin-rich syrup (it takes just three rosehips to equal the vitamin C content of a large orange). The Greeks considered the rose to be aligned with Aphrodite, the Goddess of Love, while Egyptian rulers slept on beds literally stuffed with rose petals. Christianity later took the rose for its own purposes, associating it with the Virgin Mary.

Balsamroot

As the road climbs onto drier ground above the stream corridor, the vegetation begins to change. Sage does well here, as does rabbitbrush, broom snakeweed, and balsamroot—the latter plant casting lovely yellow blooms across the hillsides from mid-May through early July. Essentially this walk traverses an ecological bridge that exists between the alpine peaks ahead and the high desert below. One minute you'll find yourself beside an enormous talus slide, pikas rushing between the scattered slabs of rock, and the next in a pocket meadow thick with grasses and wildflowers. There are beautiful Douglas firs and Engelmann spruce here, as well as curl-leaf cercocarpus—sometimes called "mountain mahogany"—and small huddles of black willow and chokecherry.

Shortly after you pass a magnificent talus slope at about 1.6 miles, the canyon begins to narrow. In another 0.2 mile you'll reach our turnaround, at the point where Cold Creek comes in from a deep ravine to the north. In the summer this makes a wonderful lunch stop, since most of the immediate area is bathed in the cool shade of spruce, fir, and aspen. Were you to walk another 2.8 miles up the trail (doing some serious climbing along the way), you'd find yourself on the spectacular Lemhi Divide. Strung together by 10,000- and 11,000-foot peaks, this craggy backbone of the Lemhi Range is pure alpine. It's a place of lingering snows, fast-stepping streams, and tiny pocket lakes—a crisp, soaring landscape, a world away from the Pahsimeroi and Lemhi valleys far below.

WALK #62—MILL CREEK LAKE

DISTANCE: 5 miles

ENVIRONMENT: Mountain

LOCATION: Challis National Forest. From U.S. Highway 93 at the tiny town of Ellis, turn southeast along the north side of the Pahsimeroi River, following a road that leads through the village of May. Follow this for approximately 53 miles to Sawmill Canyon Road, which takes off on your left. Continue for 10.2 miles, and turn right onto Forest Road 171. Proceed 0.8 mile down this road to the trailhead. Our walk is along trail 82—the Main Fork Trail, now a National Recreation Trail.

Although the 2.5-mile, 1,200-foot climb to Mill Creek Lake isn't exactly a walk in the park, the grade is in most places fairly pleasant—certainly manageable by anyone who takes time to savor the beauty along the way. This slice of the Lemhi Range is a land of stream corridors thick with vegetation, as well as vast mountains of talus sprouting ragged patches of lichen. There are cool groves of spruce and aspen and parched huddles of lodgepole pine and Douglas fir, not to mention trailside gardens peppered with larkspur, rue anemone, squaw currant, and sage.

The first stretch of this walk is through a loose weave of aspen riddled with the blooms of columbine and sticky geranium. Besides holding some of the most beautiful pink flowers you'll find anywhere in the forest (blooming here in June and July), the leaves of sticky geranium are often eaten by deer, elk, moose, and bear. Just after crossing Mill Creek, notice at 0.1 mile the large dead snag beside the trail. While many of us don't give standing dead timber a thought, it has tremendous value to wildlife. Hairy woodpeckers, for example, can often be found raising their young in large nesting cavities 10 to 20 feet off the ground, which they excavate from wood softened over time by fungi. Once the woodpecker family moves out, the hole may be taken over by a mountain chickadee or even a saw-whet owl, a fairly approachable bird that at night flies through the conifers hunting rodents. Up and down the length of

Sticky Geranium

such snags you can see holes where woodpeckers have been feeding on carpenter ants. And finally, the broken branches of snags are frequently used as perches. This snag alone may have three dozen species of birds resting on, feeding from, or hunting insects from its stubby branches at various times of the day.

After leaving the creek and climbing gently through a corridor of Douglas fir, aspen, squaw currant, and fireweed, at 0.5 mile you'll once again pick up the cool tumble of Mill Creek. When you reach this point, notice the increased variety of plants making their homes along this stream corridor. This is due not just to additional moisture, but to the greater amount of available light. Look for a classic mix of Idaho montane plants, including willow, sedge, rue anemone, cow parsnip, and saxifrage. Soon you'll leave Mill Creek again, and make a dry, fairly healthy climb along a bench paralleling the stream channel. Along the way the path makes a slow, rather delicious transition between forest and mountain, passing jumbles of talus where aspen and dwarf juniper are struggling for toeholds, as well as increasingly rugged outcroppings of rock, which frame the west side of the ravine.

Stop for breath on occasion, turn around, and drink in the view opening up to the southwest of the long, lonely Pahsimeroi Valley and the Lost River Range. The name *Pahsimeroi* is thought to be of Shoshoni origin, roughly meaning "single grove of trees near the water." Indeed, this dry, yawning reach of the Pahsimeroi Valley did at one time have but one grove of conifers standing in

Yellow-bellied Marmot

Bushy-tailed Woodrat

it, not far from the Pahsimeroi River. The first American explorer to stumble into Shoshoni homelands was a rather famous fellow named Meriwether Lewis. The people not only didn't resent the intruder, but they greeted him with bear hugs, traded horses with him, and offered no small amount of valuable advice about what lay ahead for the Lewis and Clark expedition along the Idaho's rugged rivers and mountains.

Little could those Shoshoni have known the tide of humanity that would soon follow. Fifty years later there were hundreds of wagons and livestock by the thousands crossing Indian lands nearly every summer day, decimating the range, pushing the Shoshoni to the walls of their traditional territories, beyond which they could go no farther without inflaming other tribes. During the Civil War, federal troops were few and far between; military leaders and their civilian volunteer contingents often took drastic, ruthless measures to quell the Indians. At one point, while traveling from California to Utah to protect emigrants traveling west on the wagon trails, Colonel Patrick Edward Connor developed a particularly appalling way of dealing with the angry Bannocks and Shoshoni. At the mere suggestion of robbery, kidnapping, or an attack on white settlers, Connor sent one of his men to round up every Indian he could find in the area where the incident occurred. He then sent word to their main tribe, demanding that the guilty parties be handed over. If they were not, he executed the hostages. Hundreds and hundreds of Indians were killed this way, many of whom had no part in any aggression against the whites.

By 2.1 miles the trail will have entered a flat area lined with pockets of spring water, surrounded by vast fields of talus—a great place to see pikas scurrying around the rocks. Soon afterward you'll reach Mill Creek Lake, at an elevation of 8,350 feet. This little alpine jewel lies cradled by scattered jumbles of rock, the scene spiked with Douglas fir, whitebark pine, and shaggy tufts of currant and bunchgrass.

WALK #63—LOWER FALL CREEK FALLS

DISTANCE:	2.8 miles
ENVIRONMENT:	Mountain
LOCATION:	Challis National Forest. From the Sun Valley Mall, head northeast on Trail Creek Road for approximately 22 miles to Forest Road 135 (Copper Basin Road), and turn right. *Note:* Trail Creek Road crosses Trail Creek Summit, which is not recommended for vehicles pulling trailers. Continue on Road 135 for 2.1 miles, then bear right onto Road 136. Follow this for 3.6 miles to a dispersed camping area on the right, located just past a bridge over Fall Creek. Park here, and begin your walk on the other side of Forest Road 136, on a two-track marked with the number "503."

Because the first 0.5 mile of this easy walk overlaps with the Fall Creek trek (see page 211), you may want to combine the two into a single outing. The floodplain of Fall Creek is an entirely different world than that of the high, pine-covered ridgeline traversed by our other route.

Instead of crossing the footbridge over to the north side of Fall Creek at 0.5 mile, continue straight on the small road that parallels the south side of the stream. After 0.2 mile of forest the road ends and becomes a trail, descending into a beautiful bottomland peppered with young aspen and lodgepole pine. Here and there you'll see gigantic boulders sitting among the young trees. These are known as *glacial erratics*, and they were carried from the mountains 15,000 years ago, on the cold, massive shoulders of glaciers. (Some of the rocks in this area have also been deposited by high water; we'll take a closer look at such flood-related events in a moment.)

There are two features in this region that serve as unmistakable fingerprints of glacial activity. The first are known as *moraines*, which are long ridges of gravelly debris, often covered with dryland plants such as sage, that generally mark the boundaries of glacial outflow. The second and more obvious clue is the presence of dramatic, deeply serrated peaks throughout much of central Idaho. It's hard to imagine solid rock being sculpted like so much clay, but

Central Idaho

Red-shafted Flicker

that's exactly what happened under the power of massive, 2,000-foot-thick sheets of ice. Indeed, while great uplifts along various fault lines may have been responsible for the high country ending up where it did, a great deal of the rugged, breathtaking grandeur that marks so much of these lands is thanks to the glaciers.

After 0.2 mile of lightly forested bottomland the path breaks out onto a flat sagebrush plain—a good place to look for paintbrush, larkspur, yarrow, stonecrop, blue flax, and lupine. This open area, often bathed in brilliant sunlight, lasts for about 0.4 mile, at which point the path enters a fine woodland cradling the edge of Lower Fall Creek Falls.

This is a fine little waterfall—terraces dappled with icy pools, the water pouring off the escarpments in big, broad strokes. Mosses flourish here. On the upper reaches of the cascade, conifers can be seen leaning out over the stream, giving a tattered cast to the scene that seems more reminiscent of western Oregon than of central Idaho. Even in low water this fall is impressive; in high water it can seem like the birthplace of mountain thunder.

In August of 1984 a tremendous rain fell in the Fall Creek and Wildhorse drainages—10 inches in less than half a day. This one stream swelled to an unbelievable discharge rate, sending a 25-foot-high wall of water crashing down the valley; at its peak, it was kicking out more flow than the Missouri River kicks out on the average! Rocks and trees and massive scoops of soil were torn from the banks and sent crashing down the mountains in a scene of unbelievable fury. The trail that used to ascend beyond these falls to your right was wiped out altogether. When the waters cleared

Bobcat

again, this was a much different place. Several upstream meadows were washed away completely, while steep, bare escarpments stood where only gentle hills had been before. With a flick of that single storm, the land had gone through erosional changes that would have normally taken centuries to complete.

Impressive as it was, the flood of 1984 almost pales in comparison to one that struck just 20 years earlier. This time the flood waters raged all the way to U.S. Highway 93, wiping out all the bridges along the way. Trailers, pickups, buildings, and heavy equipment at the Cordero Mine were either washed away or buried in gravel. (The mine did rebuild. Alas, their new "flood-proof" bridge floated away in the flood of 1984.) Surprise Valley Lake, which lies in a beautiful mountain valley just to the south of here, was choked with debris.

Sir Walter Scott may have been talking about Caledonia when he wrote in *Lay of the Last Minstrel* about that "stern and wild" setting, that "land of the mountain and flood." But something tells me that Fall Creek and the mighty Pioneer Range would have served him just as well.

> O Fall Creek! stern and wild,
> Meet nurse for a poetic child!
> Land of brown heath and shaggy wood;
> Land of the mountain and the flood!

Yes, I rather like that.

WALK #64—FALL CREEK

DISTANCE: 3.5 miles
ENVIRONMENT: Mountain
LOCATION: Challis National Forest. From the Sun Valley Mall, head northeast on Trail Creek Road for approximately 22 miles to Forest Road 135 (Copper Canyon Road), and turn right. *Note:* Trail Creek Road crosses Trail Creek Summit, which is not recommended for vehicles pulling trailers. Continue on Road 135 for 2.1 miles, then bear right onto Forest Road 136. Follow this for 3.6 miles to a dispersed camping area on the right side of the road, located just past a bridge over Fall Creek. Park here, and begin your walk on the other side of Road 136, on a two-track marked with the number "503."

A lot of people drive the first 0.5 mile of this route, parking at the point where a wooden footbridge crosses the stream. But the feeling that comes from walking through this yawning sagebrush steppe, Fall Creek singing beside you and the soaring Pioneer Mountains ripping into the burnt blue of a summer sky, left me no choice but to abandon the car and get down to the delights of hoofing it. In fact, if you really want to do this region right, camp for a couple days at Fall Creek Trailhead or down the road at Wildhorse Campground and walk all over the place. You can go south along Wildhorse Creek toward the magnificent ramparts of Hyndman Peak, or, if you're especially ambitious, follow the Right Fork of Fall Creek to the stunning, glacier-scoured Surprise Valley. All in all, this is a brilliant land of sage, spruce-fir forest, and fast-stepping streams—Idaho at its astounding best.

The two-track road rambles gently along the south side of Fall Creek through sagebrush, rabbitbrush, and broom snakeweed. Though such vegetation zones tend to fly by the car window in a dull blur of green, those who give them a closer look will discover a special kind of beauty. For instance, this is where you'll often find the lovely scarlet blooms of paintbrush, a plant that purposely sets up shop next to sagebrush in order to steal nutrients from its root

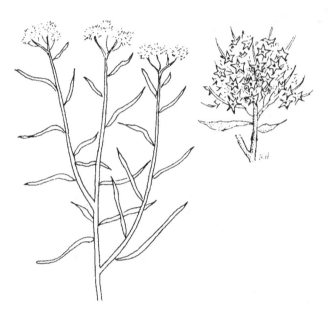

Rabbitbrush

Broom Snakeweed

system. You may also see the yellow, star-shaped blooms of stonecrop, as well as the white umbrella-blooms and fernlike leaves of yarrow. Yarrow has a wonderful history of healing. Its genus name, *Achillea*, refers to a similar plant that Achilles used to stop bleeding from the wounds of his soldiers at the battle of Troy. (A nickname for yarrow is "soldier's woundwart.") Scientists researching the chemical composition of yarrow have identified an alkaloid present named achillein, which does in fact reduce the clotting time of blood. Early Indian tribes of this region used yarrow for other medicinal purposes as well, including brewing a tea for breaking fevers and colds.

At 0.5 mile you'll cross to the north side of Fall Creek on the footbridge mentioned earlier. (Going straight will take you to Lower Fall Creek Falls; see page 208 for a description of this walk.) As you enter the mouth of the canyon you'll find old Douglas fir and whitebark pine, as well as a few clusters of aspen tucked into the lower reaches of the valley. At 1.1 miles is a fork, where you'll stay left, and begin a moderate to steep climb. Any time you're feeling winded, just turn around for a few minutes and drink in the splendid view of Hyndman Peak, Duncan Ridge, and Phi Kappa Mountain in the Pioneer Range off to the southwest. The town of Sun Valley is on the other side of that high divide, less than 20 miles as the hawk flies from where you're now standing.

While resting on the upslope you might also want to scan the trees for Clark's nutcrackers, rather large gray-and-white birds that flit through this slice of forest with great abandon. These curious, raucous birds love pine seeds, and in fact have a special pouch under their tongues to allow them to carry off several at a time. Not that they're purists when it comes to food, mind you. Nutcrackers are perfectly capable of nabbing insects on the wing, ferreting out various kinds of bugs from beneath the bark of conifers, and—perhaps their greatest talent—flying into picnic sites and helping themselves to whatever tidbits the humans have abandoned. Clark's nutcrackers are found throughout the piney mountains of the West, from southern British Columbia all the way to Baja, California.

After completing the steepest section of the climb, at 1.7 miles you'll find yourself at a fork; stay right. Our turnaround point is less than 0.1 mile from here, at a place where the path rounds the outside edge of a small hill, onto a promontory high above Fall

Clark's Nutcracker

Creek. From here, there are grand views to the west of the Pioneer Mountains, and to the east, the glaciated cirques and horns that flank the edge of the Copper Basin cowboy country. Directly below you Fall Creek has carved out several blue-green pools— a chain of brief, beautiful pauses before it tumbles on to its rendezvous first with Wildhorse Creek and then with Big Lost River to the north.

WALK #65—WEST FORK TRAIL

DISTANCE: 2 miles
ENVIRONMENT: Forest
LOCATION: Sawtooth National Recreation Area. Travel north out of Ketchum on State Highway 75 for approximately 7 miles, and turn right onto a road that runs along the east side of Sawtooth National Recreation Area Headquarters. (This road is located 0.3 mile north of mile marker 136.) Follow this for 5.4 miles to the trailhead parking lot. Two trails take off from here; our walk runs west, descending to cross the West Fork of the Big Wood River.

Though this outing will offer some rather impressive views of the craggy scarps that make up the southern edge of the Boulder Mountains, the West Fork Trail (actually the West Fork of the North Fork of the Big Wood River) isn't what most people would call spectacular. It's better thought of as a gentle meander through a mature spruce-fir forest—a loosely woven cathedral of conifers, spiked here and there by sunlit meadows of grasses, wildflowers, and currants.

The path begins with a gentle descent to the West Fork, which it then crosses on fallen logs. This is a good place to look for strawberry, rue anemone, milkvetch, monkeyflower, yarrow, sticky geranium, and, in the more open areas, paintbrush and mullein. The 2- to 6-foot-tall spikes of mullein, with their fuzzy leaves and tightly packed clusters of yellow flowers, make it one of the easiest of all plants to identify. Step up for a close look at mullein's hairy leaves, and you'll understand why it's also sometimes known as "flannel flower" or even "bunny's ears." For centuries people living in cold climates have packed mullein leaves into the bottoms of their shoes in order to keep their feet warm. In Roman times the stems were dipped in fat and used as torches, while no witch of the Middle Ages worth her cauldron would be caught without mullein as an ingredient for love potions.

Mullein also has a fairly impressive list of medical uses. Northwest pioneers, for example, found out from various Indian peoples of the region that smoking the leaves of the mullein would relieve coughs and asthma. (The plant contains large amounts of *mucilage*, a substance that helps ease irritated mucous membranes.) Mullein extracts have also been found to soften the skin, as well as to relieve minor skin irritations.

Shortly after crossing the stream the trail begins a gentle ascent through a forest that gets increasingly impressive as you make your way up the canyon. The primary spruce you'll see here is the Engelmann, which is found throughout much of the West, from central British Columbia all the way into New Mexico. This is the tree that lends luster to many of the more idyllic scenes of the Rocky Mountains. It's the tree that stands in such somber huddles along the shores of quiet, mid-elevation lakes; the tree that in winter punctuates so many of the region's open park lands, its dark, supple branches rising from thick quilts of snow. Unlike some conifers, Engelmann seedlings can live and grow in the shade of

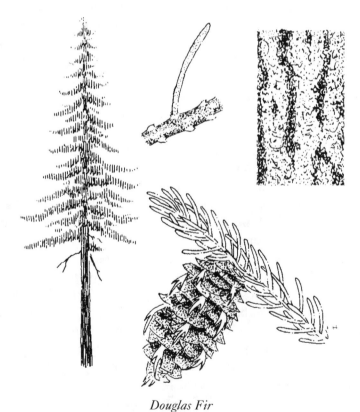

Douglas Fir

their parents, albeit slowly. When trees weakened by age or disease start falling over, the youngsters suddenly find themselves in streams of sunlight, at which point they kick into high gear.

The other common conifer keeping you company along this walk is the Douglas fir. But for the two types of sequoia found farther to the west, this is the grandest tree in all of North America. It was to the Douglas fir that the lumber industry turned at the end of the 19th century as the great stands of eastern white pine played out. When it came time to replace the masts of that great historic ship *Constitution* (*Old Ironsides*), no eastern white pine of sufficient size could be found. In the end, it was a Douglas fir that finally filled the bill. Identifying Douglas fir, which isn't a true fir at all, is relatively easy. Just take a close look at one of the cones; sticking out from between the scales will be three-pointed, trident-shaped bracts.

When botanist David Douglas first strode ashore near the Columbia River in 1825 and began measuring the species that would one day take his name, he was hardly unimpressed with the size. One fallen giant measured a whopping 227 feet long and 48 feet around! While the Douglas fir along this trail are hardly that big, several are thought to be at least 400 years old. That means these guys were poking their heads into the sun about the time a math professor named Galileo was dropping objects off the Tower of Pisa.

In about a mile the trail will have rejoined the stream again—directly across from a number of beetle-killed trees, as well as a fine avalanche slope, where young spruce and fir are already racing to reclaim the land. From here you can reach the West Fork easily, walking through the open forest, past lovely clusters of currant bushes.

WALK #66—ALPINE CREEK TRAIL

DISTANCE: 4.2 miles
ENVIRONMENT: Mountain
LOCATION: Sawtooth National Recreation Area. Heading north on State Highway 75 past Galena Summit, turn left (west) 0.5 mile past mile marker 168, following the signs to Alturas Lake. Follow this road for 6.5 miles, where it will end at the Alpine Creek trailhead.

The name Alturas, which graces the beautiful lake you passed on the way to this trailhead, at one time referred to this entire region. *Alturas* is a Spanish word that means "mountainous heights," though on occasion writers have interpreted it to mean "heavenly heights." The latter translation may be more appropriate, since this slice of Idaho is about as close to heaven as a person can get. If you came here from Ketchum and took the time while at Galena Summit to peer down the rugged line of peaks that spill northward along the Salmon River, you'd likely agree with the 1937 *WPA Guide to Idaho*, which called that view "one of the most remarkable in the West." In the 1920s people crossing Galena would sometimes tie logs onto the rear bumpers of their Model Ts to slow their descent. For years, piles of these logs were visible at the bottoms of both sides of the pass.

True to the region's reputation, this walk will take you into a stunning collage of mountainscapes, most of them cradled either by cool green forests of lodgepole, spruce, and aspen, or meadows choked with paintbrush, cinquefoil, and sage. Though there are some short, steep sections to this walk, in general the path is easily negotiated. Besides, there are plenty of mountain chickadees, Clark's nutcrackers, and even an occasional western tanager to keep you company while you catch your breath.

We'll be starting our walk in a classic lodgepole forest underlain by bright green tufts of grouse whortleberry. The lodgepole is among the most hearty and tenacious of all the pines, and the only one found in both Alaska and Mexico. True to its name, this tree did in fact form the framework for early Indian lodges, though early Europeans in the region wasted no time putting it to their own

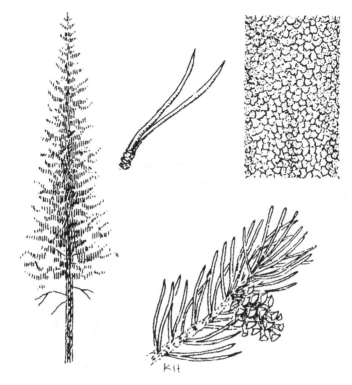

Lodgepole Pine

Western Tanager

uses. The excellent strength-to-weight ratio of lodgepole made it perfect for everything from fences to corrals to mining timbers. At just over 0.3 mile, you'll cross into the Sawtooth Wilderness, where the trail settles into a few serious climbs through a forest of lodgepole and spruce, with an occasional patch of willow. At just over 0.75 mile, where the ground is washed in the soft green of thimbleberry, the trail will come out onto the edge of a large talus slope, where willow, aspen, and dense clusters of twinberry have managed to carve out good lives among the jumble of rocks. This is a perfect place to listen for the *eeek!* of the pika, a small rabbitlike rodent that scurries about cutting grasses and drying them on slabs of rock, thus building a good store of tasty hay for the long winter ahead.

This talus slope is also a good place to look for fireweed—a tall, spindly plant that in mid- to late summer sports beautiful

Golden-mantled Ground Squirrel

Western Blue Flag Iris

lavender blossoms. Fireweed produces seeds with light, silky hairs, perfect for catching free rides on the early autumn winds. In the best of cases, those seeds end their journeys on burned or otherwise disturbed areas, reclaiming them with amazing speed. In fact, fireweed was often the first life to be seen growing among the bombed-out rubble of World War II England.

From here the path skirts glorious mountain views, occasionally passing through thin ribbons of forest. At 1.9 miles you'll reach a long swell of open land on your left that runs thick with cinquefoil, paintbrush, and various grasses all the way down to Alpine Creek. Slightly upstream from this is a wild-looking braid of beaver ponds framed by dark huddles of spruce. It was the beaver that first brought Hudson's Bay Company trapper Alexander Ross into this country in 1824—the last stop on a splendid journey among the Wood, Boise, Weiser, and Payette rivers. But alas, Ross's trip wasn't exactly an economic success. A band of Iroqouis trappers working for Ross so infuriated the Snake Indians with their high-handed "terms" (supposedly handed down by Ross himself) that the Snakes promptly robbed them on the spot. What could have been a sterling career for Ross with the Hudson's Bay Company was dashed. Even so, the journals this hearty explorer kept are among the best and most detailed to come out of the fur trade era.

Our turnaround point is at 2.1 miles, where the trail joins Alpine Creek. The maintained trail ends in another 0.4 mile. Those who are feeling especially hale and hearty can make their way cross-country over fairly rugged terrain into the lovely Alpine Lakes Basin. Good equipment and adequate maps are a must.

WALK #67—FISHHOOK CREEK

DISTANCE: 5.5 miles
ENVIRONMENT: Mountain
LOCATION: Sawtooth National Recreation Area. From the town of Stanley, head south on State Highway 75 for about 5 miles and turn west, following the signs for Redfish Lake. Approximately 2 miles down this road you'll come to a split; follow the left fork, and then make a quick right turn into the backpackers' parking area. Our walk begins on Trail 101, which first crosses the paved road that runs along the northern edge of the parking lot.

If you never quite make it out of the easy chair to another single place mentioned in this book, at least make it to the Sawtooth Valley. The lands that rise along the first 30 miles of the Salmon River—the White Cloud Peaks to the east and the Sawtooth Mountains to the west—are about as splendid as the American West gets. To walk the shores of the region's shimmering lakes, or daydream in the shadow of these rugged, weather-scoured peaks, is to find your spirit sizzling from bolts of sheer, unfettered splendor.

If you arrive at the parking area on a typical summer day, you may begin to wonder just how many other people are going to be

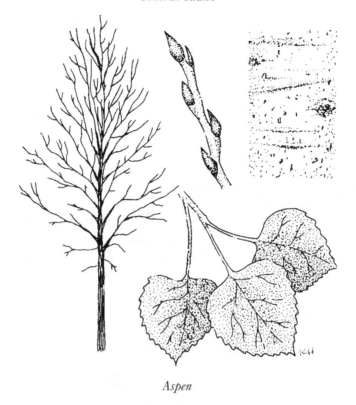

Aspen

gulping down shots of the Sawtooths at the same time you are. Don't worry. The first stretch of this pathway serves people going to Marshall Lake or up the north shore of Redfish Lake, which is also a beautiful walk. Things will have quieted down considerably by the time a mile passes underfoot.

By 0.15 mile the lovely, fast-stepping waters of Fishhook Creek will be on your left, framed by lodgepole, fireweed, lupine, paintbrush, and tufts of aspen and sage. This creek is a major feeder for Redfish Lake, which gets its name from the numbers of kokanee, or "landlocked" salmon that live there. At spawning time these fish turn a beautiful crimson color and begin migrating up the feeder streams toward home—laying eggs in the same place where they began life. The female lays her eggs in excavated depressions called "redds," immediately after which the male fertilizes them. Both adults then die. Essentially, this is a miniature version of the magnificent tale played out by the chinook in the Salmon River just to the east. Historically, those fish have traveled more than 900 miles upstream to their birthplaces, guided by an uncanny ability to "taste" minute amounts of their home waters in the heavy flows of the Columbia and Snake rivers.

About 0.3 mile into the walk you'll see a small footbridge on your left crossing Fishhook Creek. Immediately on the other side, off in a pocket of trees to the left, are the remains of an old grizzly bear trap built by a 19th-century trapper. The door was held open by a wooden prop, to which cording was attached that went over the length of the trap and through a hole in the back side, where it was tied to a piece of bait. Mr. Bear crawled into the trap to fetch the bait, yanked on the rope, and in the process pulled the prop from the door. At first glance you may think that the trap was much too small to hold a bear. But that was the whole idea. Had the bear been able to stand erect he could have used his powerful forelegs to tear the trap to shreds; in the crawl position, though, his legs were pinned beneath him, where they did little good. On the north side of the trap you can see a small hole where the trapper stuck in the barrel of a gun to finish off his hapless victim.

Lupine

Black Bear

At 0.5 mile is a junction with the Redfish Lake Trail. We'll continue straight, entering a fairly homogeneous lodgepole forest, the open areas to the right peppered with bunchgrass and scattered blooms of lupine and arrowleaf balsamroot. At 1 mile is a trail to Marshall Lakes; this is a very exposed pathway, and on a hot summer day it can bake the oomph right out of you. Once again we'll continue straight, along a remarkably quiet, peaceful stretch of trail. For the next 1.75 miles you'll be making a gentle meander through a vast quilt of lodgepole, Fishhook Creek gliding gently through the hush of the forest.

Perhaps it's the long walk through a landscape devoid of anything bold or remarkable that makes the view in 2.75 miles, at the wilderness boundary, seem like such a bolt out of the blue. In front of you is a thick riparian meadow, thoroughly cloaked in wildflowers and laced with beaver runs. Beyond that are the magnificent Sawtooth Mountains, their feet and shoulders wrapped in tattered blankets of spruce and fir.

Though I've been fortunate enough to have walked in almost every major mountain range in the continental United States, never have I found one that can massage the knots out of my soul better than the Sawtooths. Responding to an invitation by poet William Wordsworth to accompany him on a trek to the high country, English literary critic Charles Lamb wrote a polite letter of refusal. "Separate from the pleasure of your company," Lamb said, "I don't much care if I never see a mountain in my life." Poor Lamb! Surely he never imagined there was a place with mountains like these.

Red Squirrel

WALK #68—CROOKED RIVER

DISTANCE: 2.5 miles
ENVIRONMENT: Mountain
LOCATION: Boise National Forest. From Discovery State
Park on the east edge of Boise, follow State
Highway 21 for 48 miles to Forest Road 384,
and turn right. (This turn is east of mile
marker 56.) Follow Road 384 for just over a
mile to a small pullout on the right. (This
pullout is located at the point when you first
see the Crooked River; another clue is that
the road makes a 90-degree turn to the left.)

Beginning as a modest streamside meander through a lodge-pole forest, this path gets more intriguing with every step. In time it will carry you into a fabulous mix of rock, water, and high, rugged hills draped in forests of fir and pine. Don't be surprised if you have trouble calling it quits at the Summit Creek turnaround. Ambitious walkers can carry on, though a river crossing is required at about 1.7 miles from the trailhead.

Barely 50 steps from your car you'll cross Edna Creek, so named by miner John Henry, who was thoroughly lovesick over a woman named Edna Ashcroft. Edna was the daughter of a Boise County clerk and recorder, and, unfortunately for John, the wife of a miner from Placerville. John first named his mine for Edna, and then later gave the name to this creek. From here on, the path never strays far from the Crooked River, making a beautiful run southward past long ribbons of alder, their thin leaves twisting in the summer breeze. Beyond the banks is a quiet forest of primarily mature lodgepole; notice how in many places these trees have "self-pruned," letting lower branches that are out of the reach of sunlight slowly die away.

Taking off to the right at 0.3 mile is a new equestrian trail that winds up and around the hillsides, joining our walking path again near our turnaround at Summit Creek. We'll continue straight at this junction, crossing Lamar Creek at 0.4 mile. From here there are tantalizing glimpses of the surrounding terrain; notice the gray granite outcroppings on the edges of the valley, many of which hold the massive, cinnamon-colored trunks of ponderosa pine. A couple hundred yards past the Lamar Creek crossing, look carefully on the other side of the river for neat piles of rocks along the shore. These are the remains of ditch lines built for mining operations in the late 1880s.

By the time 1.2 miles have passed, you'll be able to look across the Crooked River into a dizzy rise of 500-foot slopes capped by sheer gray cliffs, the upper reaches smoothed and polished by wind and water. Even the stream has a decidedly wilder cast to it here, logs tangled and tossed by spring runoff into sizable jams, with massive chunks of granite that have fallen from the high ledges strewn about the center of the channel.

In 1.2 miles, past trailside patches of currant, is our turn-around at Summit Creek, which began on the timbered ridges near Mores Creek Summit. If you scan the north side of this creek, you'll see a number of granite ledges and boulders that make perfect places to lunch, nap, read, or otherwise while away the day. Look carefully, and you'll also see an old pipe twisting around the hillside here—more evidence of early mining operations. While miners typically dug ditches to feed water to their placer operations, these granite walls made that option next to impossible.

From here the Crooked River continues southeastward for another 9 miles to the Boise River, which itself is fresh from a dazzling run out of the Sawtooth Mountains. By the time the Boise joins the Snake River south of Ontario, on the Idaho-Oregon border, it will have drained 4,000 square miles of west-central Idaho; much of that land, it could be argued, ranks among the most delightful to be found anywhere in the intermountain West.

WALK #69—COTTONWOOD CREEK

DISTANCE: 2.8 miles
ENVIRONMENT: Forest
LOCATION: Boise National Forest. From Discovery State Park, on the east edge of Boise, follow State Highway 21 east for 21 miles, and turn right
  ▪ onto Forest Service Road 377. (This turnoff
  ▪ is east of mile marker 31.) The small trailhead
  ▪ parking area, located on the left side of the road, is just under 11 miles from the Highway 21 intersection.

When you're walking through this peaceful ponderosa forest, it's hard to imagine the hell-bent activity that roared up and down these gulches during the glory days of gold mining. At one time Idaho City, located just 11 miles to the north, eclipsed Portland to become the largest city in the Northwest. Within 12 months of its founding in 1862 the town swelled to nearly 6,000 people (well served by 25 saloons and 4 breweries), with another 10,000 scattered elsewhere along the 30-mile Boise Basin. This was easily the most productive gold mining district in the state of Idaho; on some claims, thousand-dollar days were not unusual. It must have been an incredible sight to step out on the streets of Idaho City late in the evening and see the hills glowing with hundreds and hundreds of pitch-pine torches, their lights allowing anxious miners to labor through the cool mountain nights.

Our walk begins above Cottonwood Creek, traversing a slope dotted with fine old ponderosa and, in spring through early summer, the striking yellow blooms of arrowleaf balsamroot. Along the first 0.25 of trail you'll see an intriguing mix of plants: those that like drier conditions, such as bitterbrush, hug the open slopes, while in shaded areas and along the stream corridor lay beautiful weaves of alder, violet, serviceberry, currant, and waterleaf. Waterleaf stores large amounts of food in its roots, which enables it to start growing quickly in the spring, when moisture is at its peak. The plant gets its name from the way rainwater accumulates in the pockets of the leaves.

The trail continues a gentle rise to the east, passing impressive outcroppings of pale gray granite, most of it 70 to 90 million years old. In just under a mile you'll reach a beautiful flat, open area next to the water on the left side of the trail, and immediately afterward, cross Cottonwood Creek on a wooden bridge. Pause on the bridge for a moment, and notice how different the vegetation is along the stream corridor than what you've been seeing on the trail so far. Here, for example, is the graceful mountain alder—long a welcome sight to western explorers, since it always marked the location of accessible water. Also nearby is red-osier dogwood, its stems lending streaks of crimson to the banks of the creek.

From this bridge the trail enters a narrow, rocky, and in places highly eroded canyon, passing nice gardens of false Solomon's seal, horsetail, alder, mountain maple, red-osier dogwood, and twisted stalk. At 1.4 miles you'll reach our turnaround point, at a second bridge crossing Cottonwood Creek. Those who aren't ready to stop can continue on, reaching in another 1.6 miles some fine picnic spots on the banks of Basket Springs Creek. If you really want to do this canyon right, get someone to drop you off at Thorn Creek Butte Lookout, and then walk the almost 10 miles downstream to Forest Road 377 (the road you parked on for this walk). The views to the west during this descent are wonderful, the world tumbling toward the high desert across a rumpled line of pine- and spruce-covered hills.

Southeastern Idaho

WALK #70—SAND DUNES TRAIL

DISTANCE: 5 miles
ENVIRONMENT: Desert
LOCATION: Bruneau Dunes State Park. Eastbound on Interstate 84, take exit 90, and follow Business Route I-84 toward Mountain Home. When you reach State Highway 51, go south for approximately 18 miles, and turn left (east) onto State Highway 78. The entrance to Bruneau Dunes State Park is 1.7 miles east of this junction, on the south side of the road. (Westbound on Interstate 84, take exit 112 to Hammett; then follow Highway 78 for 15 miles to the park entrance.) Follow the entrance road for just over a mile to the park visitor center; our walk takes off from here. *Note:* Always fairly strenuous, this route can be very hot during the summer months. If you plan to hike then, start your trip early in the morning and carry plenty of water. Trail brochures can be obtained in the visitor center, and are strongly recommended.

The Sand Dunes Trail at Bruneau Dunes State Park is one of those wonderful walks that takes the 20th century right out of you. To wander from wooden post to wooden post across a vast slice of trackless high desert, mats of rippling cheatgrass underfoot and the burn of a blue sky overhead, is to leave your troubles far behind. If the sheer vastness of this place doesn't get to you, then the slink of a coyote or the flash of a black-tailed jackrabbit probably will. Admittedly, this is a fairly strenuous walk, especially if you climb the crest of the dunes instead of walking around the base. But if you let your foot off the gas a little, if you waltz across this place instead

Black-tailed Jackrabbit

of race, you'll discover an amazing mix of sights, sounds, and smells along the way.

To understand the dynamics of these dunes, which are among the largest on the continent, we'll need to turn back the clock. To begin with, the sheltered pocket that holds the sands of Bruneau Dunes—a place called Eagle Cove—is the result of a river meander, cut by the Snake 2.5 to 3 million years ago. Wind blowing across the sand-laden plains carried particles of dark-colored basalt and light quartz into the cove, a process that continues to this day. But about 15,000 years ago, the north shore of a huge, 600-cubic-mile glacial lake broke and caused massive flooding through southern Idaho. Most geologists are certain that such floodwaters, which in places flowed 600 feet deep, would have washed away any sand lying in Eagle Cove; thus, the dunes you see are thought to have taken shape since that time.

As previously mentioned, much of the Sand Dunes walk doesn't follow a path per se, but rather a series of wooden posts erected in the desert. (The section of the walk back toward the visitor center can be rather tricky for first-time visitors since the posts blend in fairly well with the background.) At 1.8 miles you'll gain your first glimpse of the lake at the feet of Bruneau Dunes. This cool water shimmering in the desert is not only beautiful, but it also provides excellent habitat for a variety of water and marsh birds. The surprising part is that it got here by accident. Irrigation dams built along the Snake River caused the water table to rise, creating in 1950 the lake and marsh areas before you. Today the park maintains these areas through pumping. The most notable consequence of such watering is that, because it allows plants to grow that would otherwise not be here, what were once dynamic, changing dune fields are slowly being fixed in place.

From this point you have a choice of routes. You can climb the 470 feet to the crest of this 600-acre dune complex, pass the large crater at the top, and then drop down to the east side of the lake, or simply work your way along the south shore of the water, keeping the dunes above you. Yet another option is to cut across the strip of land between the ponds and the west side of the lake—an area thick with tamarisk, scouring rush, Russian olive, and bulrush—and rejoin the Sand Dunes loop near the picnic grounds. (This latter route will cut about 0.5 mile off your walk.) No matter which route you choose, spend as much time as you can around the lake and ponds. Depending on the season, you may see great blue herons, avocets, terns, coots, and northern harriers. This latter bird, formerly called a marsh hawk, is especially fun to watch since it will often let loose with the most amazing free-form display of rolls, dips, and loops. Some people refer to these antics as "sky dancing"—a term that seems wonderfully appropriate. Northern harriers hunt both by day and night, flying low along the edges of these marshes, eyes peeled for an unsuspecting mouse, vole, or kangaroo rat.

Bruneau Dunes is the kind of place that grows on you the more you visit. Listening to the autumn clatter of waterfowl on the lake, watching soft yellow moonlight pour into the ripples of the dunes, or catching sand lily, primrose, beeplant, and penstemon blooms spilling colors across this landscape—all are experiences not soon forgotten. What at first may have seemed a harsh, even overwhelming place begins to show its soft side, pointing to the secrets that only deserts can reveal.

WALK #71—BRUNEAU CANYON

DISTANCE: 2 miles
ENVIRONMENT: Desert
LOCATION: Bureau of Land Management. Leave Interstate 84 at either exit 90 or 99, following Business Route I-84 toward Mountain Home. When you reach State Highway 51, head south for approximately 21 miles to the town of Bruneau. Turn left (south) here onto Hot Springs Road. In 16 miles you'll see the entrance road to Bruneau Canyon Overlook on the right; turn here, and follow the road for 3.2 miles to the viewpoint.

Despite ongoing low-level flyovers by the Air Force, this is one of those marvelous, little-known gems of the American West that offer visitors a sense of personal discovery—of finding a place that, at least for a few hours, seems all your own. Of course, it's precisely these kinds of areas that seem to be regularly commandeered for bombing ranges, nuclear waste sites, and other projects that generally abuse the desert ecosystem. My best advice to you at this point is to visit the canyon as early as possible. And if you can, do it early in the morning or else late on a summer evening, when the drone of jets will have died away, and the air will be filled with nothing but the roar of the Bruneau River Rapids far below.

Besides the sheer splendor of Bruneau Canyon, this gorge has a fascinating tale to tell about the geological history of the Snake River Plain. The walls of this canyon are actually the interior of the mighty Bruneau-Jarbridge Volcano—a caldera that spewed ash over hundreds of square miles roughly 15 million years ago. You don't see the caldera today because it was eventually filled in with ash, and later, with thick flows of basalt lava. Some geologists consider this to be the beginning of the great Yellowstone eruptions—events in which a vast plain of rock was created from matter belched from the earth, later to be sculpted by the Snake River into the long line of enchanted canyons and rich riparian areas you see today.

Mountain Lion

Within this complex web of fractured volcanic rock, covered with its thin green skin of sage, is a vast underground aquifer. That said, though—contrary to opinions held by the Los Angeles County Board of Supervisors, who are routinely overcome by delusions of diverting Snake River water to Los Angeles—there is little surplus water to be had; indeed, many consider the Snake River and its aquifers to be grossly overbudgeted already.

At first glance, it might seem that these remote, rocky folds and sheer cliffs would make this a perfect place for nesting raptors. And indeed, prairie falcons, kestrels, golden eagles, and red-tailed and ferruginous hawks do sometimes nest here. But they're not as common as in the Snake River Birds of Prey Area to the northwest, which supports one of the largest concentrations of nesting raptors in the world. One reason for the difference is that this area lacks a good mix of the native shrubs and grasses that provide homes for mice, ground squirrels, voles, and rabbits—all of which are regular fare for raptors. (Managers at Snake River Birds of Prey have gone so far as to seed sagebrush in an effort to bring back dwindling jackrabbit populations; this decline is thought to be a major factor in the current low populations of nesting eagles.)

This walk is a completely free-form ramble along the rim of Bruneau Canyon. You can stroll for several miles in either direction, often without seeing another person. Access into the canyon is extremely limited; the only trail in the area—and a rugged one at that—is about 3 miles upstream from the overlook. Even if you do nothing but sit on the rim of the canyon and gaze into the wild reaches below, you'll be glad you made this trip. This is a special place, perhaps made all the more precious by the constant threats to its integrity.

WALK #72—MALAD GORGE

DISTANCE:	2 miles
ENVIRONMENT:	Desert
LOCATION:	Malad Gorge State Park. From Interstate 84 west of Twin Falls, take exit 147 and follow the signs to Malad Gorge State Park. Our trail takes off beside a large outdoor interpretive area near the Devil's Washbowl, on the east end of the park.

Located barely a good hop and a skip from Interstate 84, Malad Gorge doesn't at first appear to be exactly a pocket of tranquillity. But thanks to the sights and sounds of the Malad River as it makes a roaring 60-foot plunge over a lip of basalt into the Devil's Washbowl, it won't be long before you forget all about the drone of civilization. Besides being a good cure for the 500-miles-a-day driving blues, this walk serves as a great introduction to the complex workings of water, both on and beneath the Snake River Plain. (The Snake River Plain aquifer is one of the largest in the world; the springs in Malad Gorge alone produce a million acre-feet of water every year.)

Springs occur in this region because the Malad and Snake rivers have cut below the water table. Still, the height of the springs is such that we tend to see more of them along the canyon walls during winter, when the river is low, then during the high runoff of spring and early summer. By seeking out weak zones in the rock, these springs are actually helping to excavate this and other nearby gorges. It's thanks to the near-constant 58-degree temperature of this springwater that the inflow areas are lined with such a striking flush of plant life.

Once across the bridge, make a left turn and follow the path onto a pie-shaped peninsula. At the trail junction in 0.8 mile stay to the left, walking clockwise around the point. When you reach a place where you can look into the rugged drainage just to the west, you'll see a clear, spring-fed pool, the edges stitched with bulrush, coyote willow, and goldenrod. This drainage was carved by the same backward-cutting of the Malad River that created the Devil's Washbowl.

Almost no one traveling the Oregon Trail in the early years was ever inspired to unhitch his wagon and settle on these vast, arid plains. The Shoshoni Indians, on the other hand, were living here on a permanent basis more than 7,000 years ago, fishing for salmon, collecting wild plants, and hunting big game. It seems rather a shame that so many of us are coming to appreciate the special riches held in the arms of Idaho's high deserts just as development is pushing them forever out of reach.

If you enjoy this outing, be sure to try the Woody Cove Interpretive Area, located just southwest of the park office. On this walk you'll follow a self-guided "discovery trail," which uses an interpretive brochure full of "hints" to help you locate interesting items along the way.

WALK #73—TREE MOLDS TRAIL

DISTANCE:	2.2 miles
ENVIRONMENT:	Desert
LOCATION:	Craters of the Moon National Monument. From the town of Arco, head west on U.S. Highway 20/26/93 for approximately 18 miles; you'll see the monument entrance road on the south side of the road. This is the beginning of the Craters of the Moon Loop Road—a 7-mile tour road complete with several trailheads, interpretive exhibits, and nature trails. Our walk takes off from the southernmost reach of the drive, at the parking area for the Tree Molds Trail and Craters of the Moon Wilderness. (A good introduction to this volcanic wonderland can be had at the visitor center, which will be on your left just after making the turn into the monument.)

One does not come to appreciate this strange weave of volcanism by whizzing through it in a car. Indeed, running along the Arco Highway past hundreds of square miles of basalt flows can become a little intimidating—especially during the sizzling days of midsummer. This is one place where even cautious drivers can't help but put the pedal to the metal, in a mad dash to the shady streets of Carey. Yet, when you stop the car and start walking through these buckles and spatter cones and lava caves, you discover a world with its own brand of enchantment. This is especially true in spring, when the monument is peppered with dwarf monkeyflower, bitterroot, arrowleaf balsamroot, mock orange, dusty maiden, eriogonum, and larkspur. There are, in fact, more than 200 species of native plants growing within the borders of this monument.

As you begin this walk, to your left will be Broken Top, while farther ahead and also on the left is Big Cinder Butte—at 6,515 feet, the highest cinder cone in Craters of the Moon. Rather than being made up of lava from one giant volcano, the area before you is part of what geologists commonly refer to as the Great Rift—a 50-mile-long band of vents and fissures running to the southeast. Covering more than 600 square miles, this is the largest primarily Halocene lava field in the continental United States. Things really started happening along the Great Rift about 15,000 years ago, and thus far the zone has managed to cough up at least eight major eruptions. The last of these was only about 2,200 years ago, which makes this the most recent active volcanic site anywhere along the 400-mile Snake River Plain. Given the record of these eruptions, it wouldn't be stretching things to suggest that another eruption may not be far in the offing.

At about 0.2 mile into the walk you'll pass a small crater on the right side of the trail. To understand why this crater is here, we need to take a closer look at the stages of a volcanic eruption. Back when this land was all a flat volcanic plain, lava from deep within a magma chamber started throwing debris into the air not out of a hole, but out of a long crack, or fissure, in the earth. These initial eruptions formed lines of hot volcanic debris, sometimes called "curtains of fire," that spewed hundreds of feet into the air. As the eruption continued, part of the fissure line began to seal off as the ejected lava cooled over the top of it. After a time, instead of coming out in a continuous line of eruption, the lava was coming out of several isolated vents. More and more of those cracks were sealed off, until finally all of the lava was coming out of a single large vent.

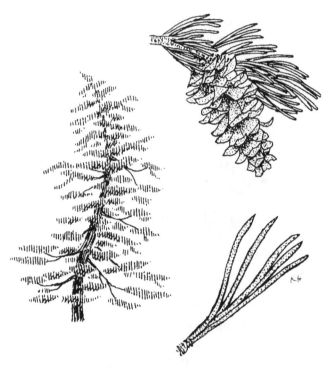

Limber Pine

Lava blowing out of that one remaining vent was charged with tremendous quantities of gas. The pressure of the gas sent a single column of very frothy lava spewing out of the ground high into the air. When it reached its apex it began to fall, in what can best be described as a "rainstorm" of cinders; cinders slowly began building around the vent, creating a cinder cone. (The size of that cinder cone was determined both by how long the eruption lasted and by how much lava was blown out.) Whether or not such cones end up with craters in them—as the one beside you did—depends on two things. First of all, if that towering column of erupting lava stops quickly, then it tends to fall back on itself, carving out a depression in the process. If, on the other hand, the eruption dies out slowly, then the vent will fill itself in, and no crater will be seen. Also, if it's very windy at the time of the eruption, you may end up with an elliptical crater, since the wind tends to blow the cinders away from the vent opening.

A short distance past this crater are some fine limber pines— rather small, twisted trees with rough brown bark. They sport five needles in each bundle, growing from branches that are often so limber they can be tied in a knot. (Please don't try this.) This flexibility comes in handy at high altitudes, when high winds can rip through the trees' branches with brutal force, and heavy snows weight them down for months at a time. Speaking of wind, as you pass these hearty trees, stop for a moment and listen to the sound made by fingers of wind running through the short needles. It's a wonderful refrain, and it goes a long way in easing the harshness of the stark lava fields to the west.

The mountains you see slightly behind you and off to your right are the Pioneers—Idaho's second highest range. Lying just east of Ketchum-Sun Valley, they are spectacular mountains, highly glaciated and thick with alpine meadows, cirque lakes, and cool huddles of subalpine fir.

In 1.1 miles you'll reach our turnaround point, at a cluster of tree molds. As the sign near the trailhead explained, these are not molds per the "thing" growing on your shower curtain; rather, they're castings of ancient trees, made when they were overrun with lava flowing at 2,000 degrees Fahrenheit. As the trees burned they released steam, which cooled the surface of the lava enough such that an impression of the tree trunk was permanently cast. There are both horizontal as well as vertical tree molds.

As you walk back, notice that some of the lava flow next to the trail has a bluish cast. This is part of what's referred to as the Blue Dragon flow. The colors result from the glassy surface of the flow, which contains thousands of tiny crystals that reflect blue light back to the viewer. Like the tree molds and the wildflowers that seem to shout out colors from the cracks in the rock, the hue of the Blue Dragon is just one more delight waiting for you in this yawning stretch of black basalt.

WALK #74—CRESS CREEK NATURE TRAIL

DISTANCE: 1.1 miles
ENVIRONMENT: Desert
LOCATION: Bureau of Land Management. From Idaho
Falls, head east on U.S. Highway 26. About
10 miles out of town, turn left (north), following the signs for Heise Hot Springs and
Cress Creek Nature Trail. (This turn is 0.3
mile past mile marker 352.) Follow this road
north for 2 miles, turn right (east) for 1.4
miles, and then left (north) for 1.2 miles to
the trailhead.

This fine little nature trail not only meanders along the shady banks of Cress Creek but also leads you high above the lazy green meanders of the Snake River—steeping you in that magical mix that occurs when arid lands and riparian zones meet. Here you'll find the hot, spicy smell of sage and the cool yellow blooms of monkeyflower, the hiss of wind and the gurgle of water. The Bureau of Land Management has produced a fine interpretive brochure keyed to numbered posts along the trail, which will help you learn many of the more common plants of the area; additional interpretive projects are underway.

After a short, steep scramble up a dry slope peppered with juniper and tufts of crested wheatgrass, you'll come to the lush banks of Cress Creek. This is a perfect place to look for watercress, the perennial aquatic plant that lends its name to this delightful little stream. Watercress was actually introduced from Europe, brought here by early settlers who knew that its high vitamin C content prevented scurvy. The plant also contains significant levels of vitamins A, B, B2, D, and E, and was once a popular ingredient in spring herbal tonics.

Continue climbing through a dry, pungent mix of rabbit-brush, bitterbrush, squawbush, juniper, and sage, with stalks of cheatgrass, buckwheat, paintbrush, and bluebunch wheatgrass rounding out the vegetation mat. As you climb, scan the sky for glimpses of bald eagles, which are frequently sighted here. (Ten pairs of bald eagles nest along a 50-mile stretch of river between

Golden Eagle

Palisades Dam and Twin Bridges. Fully half of Idaho's bald eagle productivity occurs in the region as a whole.) Another less common bird you may catch a glimpse of is the golden eagle. Because this bird's diet consists of large rodents, especially rabbits, when the sagebrush communities that rabbits live in are cleared for agriculture, golden eagle populations usually suffer. Though the shape of a golden eagle in flight is very similar to that of certain hawks, the easiest way to distinguish between the two is by the much larger wingspan of the adult eagle—typically from 6 to 7 feet across. A third large bird in the area, one that can soar with the best of them, is the turkey vulture. While mature golden eagles have an overall dark brown look, the turkey vulture sports a band of dark gray flight feathers capped by a black wing lining.

There are wonderful views along the high line of this trail, the finale coming in 0.5 mile at marker post 20, above the meanders of the mighty Snake River. Beginning along the Continental Divide in Yellowstone Park (just a short ways to the northeast from where you stand), the Snake traces a rugged route through both mountains and deserts before finally joining the Columbia, more than a thousand miles from where it began. An old river, the Snake has had to do battle with hundreds of miles of volcanic rock in order to make its way across southern Idaho, and then cut northward through basalt, diorite, granite, limestone, gneiss, and schist to carve Hells Canyon—the deepest gorge in America.

The Snake and its tributaries played an extremely important part in the development of the American West. Unable to divvy up the Northwest in an equitable manner, Great Britain and the United States agreed to occupy the area jointly for a period of 10 years. Immediately after this agreement was reached, the British increased fur trapping in the area to a fevered pitch—a pitch that some historians feel was intended to utterly deplete the supply of beaver, thus forcing the Americans to stay on the east side of the Rockies or in the Southwest. By the late 1820s it became painfully apparent that the British effort was working; most of the easy-to-reach beaver in Idaho had been thoroughly trapped out, and the Americans had to settle for better opportunities on the other side of the Tetons. For their part, Americans thought nothing of taking every beaver they could get their traps on, never giving a thought to sustaining the resource for the years ahead. Indeed, while it may have been a change of fashion that doomed the value of beaver pelts, it was the trapping companies themselves that doomed the supply.

At 0.9 mile you'll find yourself back at the point where you got your first good look at Cress Creek. Soak up the lush weave of vegetation and the chorus of birdsong one last time, and make your way down the dusty trail back to the parking lot.

WALK #75—SOUTH FORK TRAIL

DISTANCE: 3.8 miles
ENVIRONMENT: Forest
LOCATION: Targhee National Forest. From Idaho Falls, head east on U.S. Highway 26. About 18 miles out of town, turn left (north) onto Heise Road, following the signs for Heise Hot Springs. (This turn is 0.3 mile past mile marker 352.) Follow this road north for 2 miles, and turn right (east) for 1.4 miles. Turn right again here, and pass by Heise Hot Springs Resort. Two and a half miles from this last junction you'll turn right once again onto Forest Road 206 (also known as Snake River Road). Follow Road 206 for 13.3 miles (it makes a jaunt to the right at 8.1 miles), and then bear right at a "Y" intersection, following the signs for Black Canyon. Our trailhead is 1.8 miles from the "Y" intersection, on the right side of the road.

The Snake River will accompany you for much of the drive to this trailhead, offering several places to pull off and soak up the roll of mountain water, the honk of Canada geese, and the gentle flutter of aspen, willow, and cottonwood. In fact, if you're not in a hurry, you may find that the drive to South Fork Trail is one of the more engaging aspects of the entire trek.

This is one of the last places where the Snake—fresh out of Wyoming—can be considered a high-country river. Though it has so far kept close company with some of the most beautiful mountains in the West, a half-dozen or so miles downstream it will begin to settle into a long, haunting mosaic of high desert—a swath of sand and sage and basalt that frames its banks all the way to its confluence with the Columbia.

The Northern Shoshoni Indians, who once occupied much of southern and eastern Idaho, western Wyoming, and northeastern Utah, have a wonderful myth to explain the origin of the Snake River. One day, that clever trickster Coyote was out walking in the Yellowstone country when he came upon an old woman (Mother

Coyote

Earth) with a giant basket of water filled with fine fish (Yellowstone Lake). "I'm so hungry," he said in his saddest, most pathetic voice. "Won't you cook some fish for me?" The woman agreed, but before she set off to do the task, she warned him not to touch the basket. Of course, Coyote couldn't behave himself, and before long he'd managed to knock the container over, sending water and fish sprawling all over the place.

Coyote ran ahead of the water as fast as he could, trying to stop it by piling rocks in its path. But when he did, the water simply broke through his makeshift dams—first creating Upper, and then Lower Yellowstone Falls, and eventually the entire Yellowstone River. Next Coyote ran to another channel of spreading water and tried to stop it the same way. Time after time he piled up rocks in the path of the water, but each time the torrent broke through, creating what we know today as Idaho Falls, American Falls, Twin Falls—even Hells Canyon. Because of these great waterfalls that Coyote created, over which no fish can pass, salmon are no longer found along the upper regions of the Snake River. (Curiously, many geologists believe there were times when Yellowstone Lake did in fact drain into the Pacific via the Snake River, instead of into the Gulf of Mexico by way of the Missouri and Mississippi, as it does today.)

A less complicated explanation of how the Snake River came into being concerns Paul Bunyon. One night, after drinking nine kegs of rum, Paul went tottering off into the dark of night, stomping out the crazy meanders of the Snake River channel along the way.

Our trail begins by crossing Black Canyon Creek, after which it begins a fairly steep 0.3-mile climb to a saddle separating the parking area from the Snake River Valley. On both sides of this saddle you'll see places where people have "cut switchbacks," a habit that leads to serious erosion problems. Since most of the topsoil has already been washed away, it will be years before plants can stabilize these troughs.

At the top of the saddle is a striking view of the Snake River—a lush tapestry of willow- and cottonwood-lined channels, each thick with various kinds of songbirds and waterfowl. The cottonwoods here are especially significant, forming one of the most extensive forests remaining in the entire West.

One of the birds that's especially easy to see here in early summer is the Canada goose. Once the female arrives at an appropriate breeding area, such as these quiet river channels, she will direct the search for a good nest site, the male following close behind. Once a suitable place is found, the female spends the next several hours hollowing out a shallow depression in the earth and lining the perimeter with grasses, twigs, etc. (In some areas Canada geese nest on tall stumps, or in specially constructed elevated breeding boxes.)

Roughly one egg per day is laid until the entire clutch, four to six eggs, is complete. The hatch takes 28 days, and whenever the female leaves the eggs to feed, she first covers the next with leaves, feathers, or twigs. Once the kids are up and about, which takes only about 72 hours, the loud, raucous honking and posturing by the male in defense of the nest comes to an end.

In midsummer adult Canada geese go through a molt that renders them unable to fly for several weeks. As you might imagine, the birds are much harder to spot then, preferring to stay in secluded locations, dashing for cover whenever they detect the slightest threat. About the time the molt ends the young geese are able to fly, and at that point the family comes together with other families in open feeding grounds.

Canada geese mate for life, and return from their wintering areas to the same breeding grounds year after year. The internal map that leads these birds back and forth across thousands of miles is imparted by parents to their offspring in just a single migration.

Our path descends through a blend of serviceberry, bitter-brush, sage, larkspur, juniper, and arrowleaf balsamroot, framed by high, rugged cliffs and parapets chiseled out of volcanic rock. Once you've completed the short descent, the path heads east on a lazy meander through a mix of deciduous and coniferous trees under-lain with shortleberry, wallflower, and Oregon grape, the whisper of the Snake River close by. In 1.1 miles you'll cross a small cattle guard; 0.2 mile later is our turnaround, at a point where the trail opens up into a flat, open park land studded with juniper and cottonwood. Immediately across from this point is a sizeable river island—a perfect place, at least in early summer, to see the comings and goings of Canada geese.

· Suggested Reading ·

Aikens, C. Melvin. *Archaeology of Oregon*. Portland, Oreg.: U.S. Department of Interior, Bureau of Land Management, 1986.

Benyus, Janine. *The Field Guide to Wildlife Habitats of the Western United States*. New York: Fireside, 1989.

Bluestein, Sheldon. *Exploring Idaho's High Desert*. Boise, Idaho: Challenge Expedition Company, 1988.

Brogan, Phil. *East of the Cascades*. Portland, Oreg.: Binfort and Mort, 1977.

Craighead, Davis. *The Peterson Field Guide to Rocky Mountain Wildflowers*. Boston: Houghton Mifflin, 1963.

Jolley, Russ. *Wildflowers of the Columbia Gorge*. Portland, Oreg.: Oregon Historical Society Press, 1988.

Lavender, David. *Land of the Giants*. Lincoln: University of Nebraska Press. 1979.

Little, Elbert L. *The Audubon Field Guide to North American Trees*. New York: Alfred A. Knopf, 1980.

Lyons, C. P. *Trees, Shrubs, and Flowers to Know in Washington*. Oshawa, Canada: Alger Press, 1977.

McConnaughey, Bayard, and Evelyn McConnaughey. *Pacific Coast*. New York: Alfred A. Knopf, 1985.

Peattie, Donald Culross. *A Natural History of Western Trees*. Lincoln: University of Nebraska Press, 1980.

Sullivan, William L. *Exploring Oregon's Wild Areas*. Seattle: The Mountaineers, 1988.

Whitney, Stephen. *The Pacific Northwest*. Sierra Club Naturalist's Guide. San Francisco: Sierra Club Books, 1989.

Various Authors. *Roadside Geology Series*. Missoula, Mont.: Mountain Press Publishing.

· Index ·